The Harper & Row Basic Reading Program

All through the Year

by Mabel O'Donnell

Byron H. VanRoekel, *Educational Consultant*

Illustrated by Beatrice Darwin

HARPER & ROW, PUBLISHERS

Evanston, Illinois   Elmsford, New York   Pleasanton, California   New York, New York

Contents

Acknowledgment

Grateful acknowledgment is hereby given for permission to include in the illustrations on the cover and on pages 1, 189, and 191 the figure, in snow, of the dog SNOOPY from PEANUTS—Copyright by United Feature Syndicate, Inc.

The Best Detective

Helping Yourself with New Words

Picture Dictionary

bicycle

dog

doghouse

garage

step

Words You Can Get by Yourself

mad	moon	sheep	inside
sad	soon	keep	beside
		keeps	
may	will	skate	surprise
say	still	skater	surprising
for	back	is not	stop
or	track	isn't	stopped
give	round	do not	be
live	found	don't	Being
	Daddy	moon light	
	Dad	moonlight	

poked	see	but	Miss
poke	seem	cut	Mr.
joke	seemed	cutting	Mrs.
joking			

and	grandmother	long
grand	grandfather	belong
		belonged

Let the Sentences Help You

Can you answer this question?

Ann does not know the answer.

Now you ask me a question.

asks asked

I had a hamburger for my lunch.

Ann and I are going to the show.
Do you want to go with us?

Mark had two dimes, and so had I.
Together we had four dimes.

This old can is brown and rusty.

Rusty

Can you count to 100?

counting

Put your cap on your head.

Today is Saturday.
Tomorrow will be Sunday.

Do not tell anyone what I said.
It is a secret.

This apple is not big enough.
I want a great big one.

Our house is sold. We have to move.

moved   moving

You look happy when you smile.

smiled

Let the Syllables Help You

detective	whisper	never
de tec′tive	whis′per	nev′er
	whispered	

I Want to Be Best

Janet sat on the step
with her head in her hands.
She was looking as sad
as three wet days.
Daddy stopped his car
in front of the house,
but Janet did not look up.

"All right," said Daddy,
as he sat down beside her.
"Tell me all about it.
Then you will feel better."

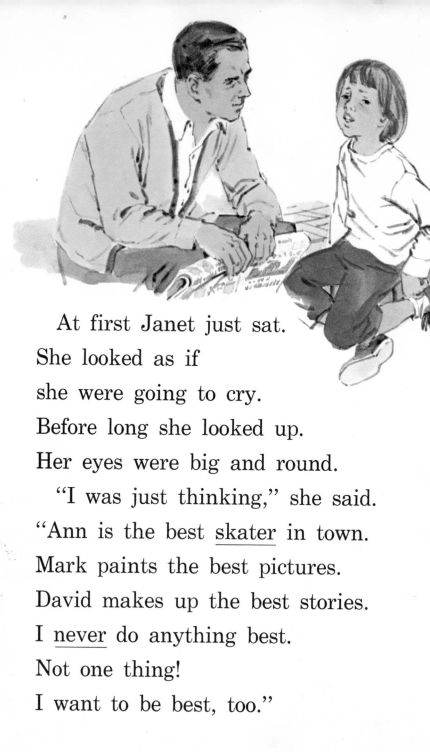

At first Janet just sat.
She looked as if
she were going to cry.
Before long she looked up.
Her eyes were big and round.

"I was just thinking," she said.
"Ann is the best skater in town.
Mark paints the best pictures.
David makes up the best stories.
I never do anything best.
Not one thing!
I want to be best, too."

"Now see here," said Daddy.
"You are my best girl.
Isn't that enough for you?"

"No, it isn't," said Janet.
"I want to do something best.
I want Mark and Ann and David
to know I am best.
I want them to say so, too."

"So you have to be best
in something," said Daddy.
"What can that something be?"

He sat on the step,
thinking and thinking.

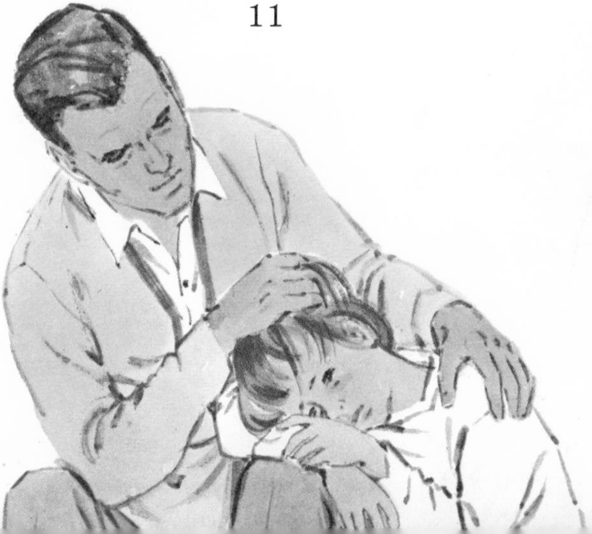

Then, all at once,
Daddy started to smile.
"You never can tell," he said.
"I may have the answer
to that hard riddle.
When Mother lost her earrings,
who found them for her?"
"I did," said Janet.
"When Mark lost his quarter
in the grass,
who found it for him?"
"I did that, too," said Janet.

"You will make
a good detective," said Daddy,
with a big, big smile.
"A better detective
than Mark or David or Ann!
You know how to stick to things
until you find out the answers.
Here come the rest of them now.
Don't tell them what I said.
Don't you let on."

Ann and Mark and David
came flying up the walk.

Tomorrow or Someday Soon

"Well, now," laughed Daddy. "How did you happen to show up just at the right time? I was just going to make a detective out of Janet. Now maybe I can make detectives out of all of you."

"Detectives! Like the ones on TV?" shouted Mark. "Boy, is this going to be fun. Come on, Dad! Start talking! No girls can be in on this. Just boys! Just David and I!"

"If that is the way you feel, just run along," said Daddy. "Girls can be good detectives. Better than some boys I know!"

Mark did not run along, and you know why. He did not want to miss out on the fun.

"Now listen to me," said Daddy. "Some people just moved into that new house on the corner."

"An old man and an old lady moved in there," said Ann. "Mother went to call on Mrs. Wells."

"Something surprising
will happen at that house soon,"
Daddy went on. "Maybe not today!
Maybe not tomorrow,
but someday soon!
The one who finds out
the surprising thing first
will be the best detective.
Now, a good detective
keeps his head about him.
He finds things out for himself.
He never asks anyone for help.
Can you three do that?
If you can, skip along.
I want to talk to Janet."

I Am Counting on You

"Now see here, young lady,"
said Daddy, with a big smile.
"I am counting on you.
Stay here with me
until those three
grow tired of looking.
Stay here with me
until they all give up.
Then you can go looking
all by yourself."

Before long Ann and David
ran home to lunch.
Mark ran into the house
and shut the door.

"No luck today!" he shouted.
"Mr. and Mrs. Wells
went away in the car."

After lunch
Janet walked up to the corner.
She stayed there a long time.
Not one thing happened.
Being a detective
all by yourself was not much fun.

Then all at once
Janet had the feeling
that the house was talking to her.

"A head is to think with,"
it seemed to say.
"Don't you see how big I am?"

"You are much too big
for just two people," said Janet.
"Is someone else moving into you?
Is that the surprising thing
that is going to happen?"

"Maybe it is! Maybe it isn't!"
the house seemed to say.
"Find out the rest of my story
all by yourself."

That night
Janet whispered to Daddy.
She had to tell him
what the house had seemed to say.

"GOOD GIRL!" said Daddy.
"You are on the right track,
but you have a long way to go."

How did Janet feel after that?

"Maybe I was a good detective
today," she said to herself.
"But I am going to be
a better detective tomorrow."

The Big Question

The next day Ann went to town
with her mother.
So she could not be a detective.
The two boys worked at the job
off and on, but not all the time.
Janet went up to the corner,
and there she stayed.

Mr. Wells had grass to cut,
but he could cut and talk, too.
So Janet followed him around
as he worked.
Not one surprising thing happened
all day long.

The next day was no better.
By now Ann and the boys
were tired of being detectives.
Not Janet! Oh, my, no!

Today Mr. Wells was at work
in back of his house.
Janet walked around to see him.
What else did she see?
There, by the back door,
was a HOUSE. A big DOGHOUSE!
OH! OH! So this was the secret.
Now she had it. Now she knew.

"You are going to get a dog!" she shouted. "A big one, too!"

"Oh, no," laughed Mr. Wells. "I am just painting this house for someone I know. Do you want to help me paint?"

So Janet stayed and painted. All the time she had the feeling that Mr. Wells knew something he was not telling. Was he in on Daddy's secret? That was the big question. If he were, he did not say a word.

Questions and Answers

A day or two went by.
The doghouse sat
all by itself in the sun.

Then one morning Mr. Wells
was at work in the garage.
Janet went inside to talk to him.
Then what did she see?
Over in one corner was a bicycle.
A not-too-big bicycle!
Just about big enough for Janet!

"What is that doing there?"
she asked. "Can you ride on it?"

"Why not?" answered Mr. Wells. "My legs are not so long as all that. I can ride backward all around town on it."

Janet knew by his smile that he was just joking. He WAS too big, and he knew it.

That night she had three questions to ask Daddy, and here they are.

1. Why does Mr. Wells have a house too big for him?
2. Why does he keep a doghouse that does not belong to him?
3. Why does he keep a bicycle that is not big enough for him?

"GOOD GIRL!" said Daddy.
"I knew I could count on you.
You know how to put
two and two together.
Now do you see the light?
Can you answer your own questions?
What is the surprising thing
that is going to happen?"

This time Janet did not whisper.

"I think I know! I think I do!"
she shouted.

Then she smiled a big smile
and whispered the secret to Daddy.

The Three Reds

On Saturday morning
the surprising thing happened.
The boys were at David's house.
Ann was helping her mother.
Janet, the detective,
was still on the job.

Once again
Mr. Wells was cutting grass.
But who was that with him?
A BOY and a GREAT BIG DOG!
They were running all around
as if they belonged there.

A house too big for two people!
A boy, and a bicycle in a garage!
A dog, and a great big doghouse!
All you had to do
was to put two and two together.
THAT boy and THAT dog
had come here to stay.

Was that all there was
to the surprise? Oh, my, no!
That boy had red hair
just like Janet's.
That dog had red hair, too.

"Things will start to move
around here now," said Mr. Wells.
"Step over here, all three of you.
Let me get a good look at you.
Upon my word! I know
what I am going to call you.

THE THREE REDS!"

Mr. Wells started to tell Janet
that the boy was called Rusty
and the dog was called Red.
He was Rusty's grandfather.
But Mr. Wells was too slow about it.
Janet did not stop to listen.

"Come with me!" shouted Janet. "Don't ask questions. Just come!"

Down the street to Ann's house scampered The Three Reds.

"See who is going to live with Mr. Wells!" shouted Janet. "Now who is the best detective?"

"You are! You are!" said Ann.

Once again, down the street flew The Three Reds. The boys were still playing ball.

"Now who gets the blue ribbon? See what I found!" shouted Janet. "Now who is the best detective?"

What could David and Mark do?
They had to find out
about this boy and his dog.
Something had to stop Janet.

In the end she made them say,
"You are the best detective
in this town."

After that, what did she do?

"You had better look out
for us," she said. "And how!
Do you know why?
Do you want to know what we are?
Just listen to this.

WE ARE

THE THREE REDS."

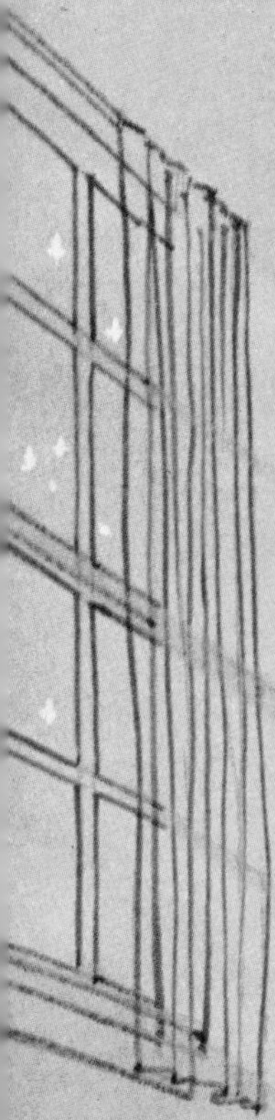

A Surprising Thing

The night was dark,
And the wind was still,
As the big round moon
Peeped over the hill.

Then a little brown bear
With a cap on his head
Came in with the moonlight
And sat on my bed.

When morning came
And the sun was out,
I looked and I looked
And I looked all about.

I looked in my room,
And I looked in my bed.
There was no brown bear
With a cap on his head.

The Hero of Spring Street

Picture Dictionary

city

postman

postmen

post office

school

Words You Can Get by Yourself

there	cake	long	postmen
where	take	wrong	post men

gate	came	not	inside
hate	blame	got	Hillside
hated	blamed	forgot	outside

hard	catbird	patted
yard	cat bird	pat
backyard		

everyone	mud	moon
Every	bud	noon
everything	buddy	noontime
Everywhere	buddies	afternoon

came	friend	David	herself
became	friendly	Dave	myself
another	left over	I am	red woods
other	leftover	I'm	Redwood
come	put	get	sun day
coming	putting	getting	Sunday

Let the Sentences Help You

My dog can wag his tail.
wagged wagging
He is a good old fellow.

You ran into our car.
It was all your fault.
Look where you are going
and keep out of trouble.

David and Mark have their bicycles.
They will wait for me
until I get my bicycle.
waited waiting

When I see someone I know, I say,
"Hi, there! How are you?"

Let the Syllables Help you

hero he′ro

I Start My Story

First I had better tell you
who I am.
I am Red, the great big dog
that lives in Redwood City.
I have a house all my own
on the corner
of Gates and Spring streets.
Look in my backyard,
and you will see it.

Rusty is the boy who belongs to me. That makes him the best boy in Redwood City. I think so. That makes me the best dog, too. That is what Rusty thinks as long as I keep out of trouble. When I make him mad, he calls me "You old dog, you!"

Before we came here, we lived in a little town called Hillside. That is where Rusty was born. We lived at the edge of town. Out there we had space enough to run and play and have fun.

It was not my fault
that we came to live in the city.
Do you know what a city is?
A city is houses and garages,
cars and people.
There is no room for anything else.
A city is where
everyone keeps on saying,
"Don't play in the street.
Don't run in front of cars.
Don't ride two on a bicycle.
Keep off the grass.
Stop, look, and listen
before you cross the street."

A city is where people say,
"There is no room around here
for a dog as big as you are.
Get out of this yard
faster than you came in!"

When I first moved to the city,
I hated it. Do you wonder why?

I live with Rusty's grandmother
and grandfather. Rusty does, too.
I do not hate them. I like them.
I like them as well as Rusty does.
Do they like me?
For a long time
that was the big question.

Every time they looked at me,
they said, "Red, old fellow!
You may be a good dog,
but why do you have to be so big?"

Now that I am a hero,
they do not feel that way.

Before I came to Redwood City,
I did not like girls.
In the city, I found one girl
I did like. She was Janet.
Her hair was red. In that way
she was like Rusty and me.
Everywhere we went,
people called us "The Three Reds."

My first days in the city
were bad, bad days for me.
What happened was not my fault.
People blamed me for everything.
First they blamed me,
then Rusty, then Janet.
Every time they saw us coming,
people called to one another,
"Look out for The Three Reds.
Now we are in for trouble."

Rusty's grandfather
wanted to trade me off for a cat.
I could not let that happen.
So what I did about it,
and how I became a hero,
is the story I am going to tell.

In the Doghouse

It all started
the morning after I moved
to Redwood City.

Rusty was still in bed.
So I went off by myself
to look things over.

Cars were starting
all up and down Spring Street.
Every man was on his way to work.
I went around wagging my tail
at all the men to show
that I wanted to be friends.

Some men smiled at me and said, "Hi, there, old fellow!"
Some men patted my head and asked, "Where did you come from?"
But there was one man who had jumped out of bed on the wrong side.

"Of all things!" he shouted. "There was trouble enough around here. Now you show up."

Was it my fault that he did not know the right side of the bed from the wrong side?

Right then and there
I stopped wagging my tail
and started to bark.
I followed him down the street,
barking my head off.
It is a wonder
I did not get run over by a car.

A boy came to the door
of a house, shouting,
"Cut it out, you! Cut it out!
My dad works nights,
and he wants to sleep."

I wanted that tired man
to have a good sleep.
So I stopped barking
and started for home.

It had rained the night before.
The rain was over,
but the grass was wet.
Was I to blame for that?

On the way home I had fun.
Dog fun! I ran up one front walk
and down the next.
Sometimes I ran
up and down the steps of the houses.
I was getting along all right
until a lady started to shout,
"Get out of here! Get!"

After that I was afraid
to run down her front walk.
So I cut across her backyard.

There I saw something white
going hop, hop, hop.
I knew at once it was a rabbit.

In Hillside, where I came from,
all the rabbits were brown.
When I saw those rabbits,
I chased them back into the woods.

People liked me for doing that.

"Good dog! Good dog!" they said.
"Let them eat their own grass.
Keep them out of our yards."

So when I saw the white rabbit,
I started right in to help out
the people on Spring Street.

I chased that white rabbit
until he ran under the house
where I could not get at him.

A little girl came out the door,
crying and crying.
After her came that same lady
with a big stick in her hand.

By the time I was back home,
the lady with the stick
had called up Rusty's grandmother.
She told her that I had chased
her little girl's rabbit.
Now they could not find it.
I had left mud tracks
all over her front steps.

Rusty's grandmother, Mrs. Wells, was saying over and over, "We will put a stop to this. You can count on that."

Then Rusty came running out in his pajamas, shouting, "You old dog, you! Boy, oh, boy! Are you in the doghouse now!"

What was he talking about? I was not in the doghouse. I was on the back steps. But before long I was where he said I was. I was in the doghouse with Grandmother's eye on me. Rusty was off to find the rabbit.

Luck in a Blue Suit

My troubles were not over at the end of that first day. Get that idea out of your head. For two or three days everything I did was wrong. But I was a smart dog. So, little by little, I learned how to live in a city.

I learned to stay in my own yard. I learned to stay out of the mud. I learned to stop barking at people I did not like. Now and then I chased a rabbit, or a squirrel up a tree. But I did it in my own yard.

What a sad time I had! I may have looked like a dog, but I did not feel like one.

There was just one time
when I could run around
outside my own yard and have fun.
That was when Rusty and Janet
were not in school.

I was their dog,
but did they let me be a dog?
They did not.
They followed me around
like two detectives
looking for trouble.
Trouble to keep me out of!

Then one morning
luck in a blue suit
came up our front walk.
That day we had a new postman
on Spring Street.

"Man, oh, man!" he whispered,
as soon as he saw me.
"Are you a beautiful dog!
For years and years
I have wanted a dog
just like you. And here you are!"

When someone likes you
as well as that and tells you so,
you know how you feel about him.
When the postman started back
down our front walk, I went, too.
That day Rusty's grandfather
was not around to shout at me,
"Get back here where you belong!"
I stayed right by the postman
to keep out of trouble.
As we walked, we talked together.
Dogs may not talk in words,
but they can talk. You know that.
Before too long, he said to me,
"Go home now, old fellow!
Someone may think
I am walking off with you."
So home I went.

The Two Buddies

Boy, will you be surprised
to hear about all the things
I learned to do next.
Don't forget! I was a smart dog.
I did not learn them all in a day.
I was smart, but not that smart.
By the time I had learned
all there was to know,
this is the way my mornings went
on every day but Sunday.

Every morning,
long before Rusty went to school,
I was off down Spring Street.
Where to? Where was I going?
To the post office!
To the branch post office
on the corner
of Park and Spring streets!

I sat on the steps
to wait for my postman to come out.
All the other postmen
who came out ahead of him
stopped to pat my head
and smile down at me.
Every one of them was my friend.

Every morning
one postman or another said,
"Why not be my buddy
and walk along with me?"

I knew he was just joking.

When I saw MY postman coming,
I wagged all over.
I waited for him to pat my head
and give me a great big smile.
Then we started on our rounds.
That is what he called them.

We walked along together
to the end of Spring Street.
We went down one side street,
then another and another.
By and by, we were right back
at the branch post office.
Then I wagged good-by
and went home.

By the time I was back home,
it was noontime and after.
Rusty was in school again,
and I was a tired-out dog.
All I wanted was a big lunch
and a long, long sleep.
When school was out for the day,
Janet and Rusty did not have to be
good detectives. Just so-so!
I was still too tired
to run around much.

Grandmother and Grandfather
were two happy people.
What did they say about all this?

"If you want to know what to do
with a big dog in a big city,
ask the postman.
Make a bargain with him
to keep your dog out of trouble."

What about the people
we saw on our rounds?
Some of them called us
"The Two Buddies."
Some of them called me
"The Postman's Dog."
One day one of them handed me
a leftover hamburger.
In no time at all
we were friends with everyone.

All in all, things seemed
to be going well with me.
I had learned to live in a city
and still be a dog.
But that did not make me a hero.
So now I will tell you about that.

Front-Page News

All the other postmen
called my postman Cap.
I don't know why, but they did.

One morning Cap and I
were on our rounds together.
All at once
a car parked in front of us,
and a man jumped out.

"Hi, there," he called,
as he walked along beside us.
"So here are The Two Buddies.
Just the ones I am looking for!"

As he walked and talked,
he started to write
in a little black book.

"I am Dave Meadows
of the 'Redwood News,'" he said.
"I'm here to get your story.
Where am I going to put you?
Right on the front page
of the Sunday paper!
I don't know who it was
who was asleep on the job.
No one told us a word about you
until a day or two ago.
Now everyone in the office
is talking about the dog
that walks the postman.
Or does the postman walk the dog?"

He stopped long enough
to give me a friendly pat.
"Out with it, Old Man," he said.
"I'm waiting for that story."
You know this, and I do, too.
I could not tell him my story.
Not in words! But Cap could.
I listened as hard as I could.
If Cap forgot something,
I poked him with my head
or my tail until he said,
"Don't let me forget to tell you
about this."
By the time we were
at the end of Spring Street,
the story was told.
"So long until tomorrow,"
said Dave, putting his book away.
Then he went back to his car.

When Cap and I came back
to the post office the next noon,
there was Dave, waiting for us.
He had come to take our picture.
Not one picture! Two or three!

That afternoon I was not tired
at all. I wonder why.
I wanted to run around all over
and tell my secret to everyone.
So maybe it is just as well
that a dog cannot talk.
Anyway not in words!

The Hero of Spring Street

Sunday is a day of rest,
but not this Sunday.
Grandfather came to the door
to get the Sunday paper.
There I was with my tail wagging.

First Grandfather looked at the paper.
Then he looked at me.

"Upon my word!" he said.
"Upon my word! Upon my word!"

He went on saying that
as if he were never going to say
anything else.

Then all at once he shouted,
"Rusty! Grandmother!
Get a move on you.
See who made the Sunday paper."

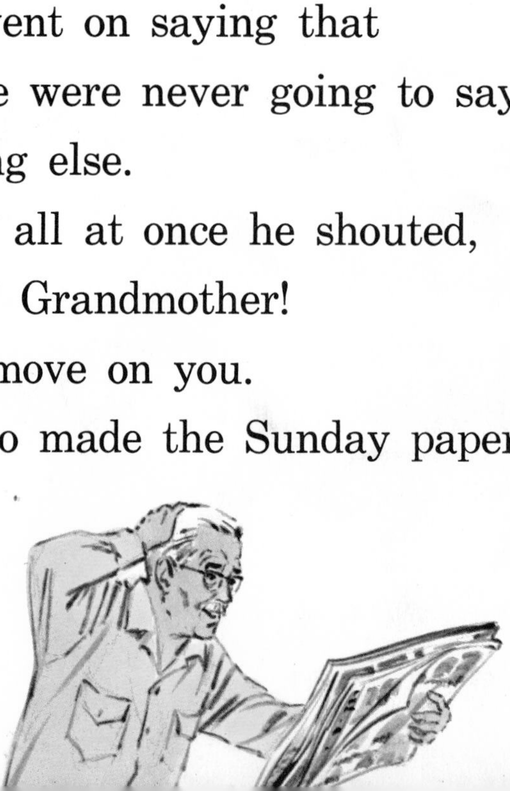

Grandmother came to the door, saying, "Don't shout so! Don't you know it is Sunday?"

But no one could stop Rusty. He laughed, he shouted, he jumped up and down.

"You look keen! Just keen!" he shouted, showing me the paper. "Red, you old dog, you! Look at yourself. Just look!"

He went right on calling me "You old dog, you," and this time I liked it.

Rusty was still in his pajamas when Janet flew in at the door with the paper in her hand.

It was not long before all the boys and girls on Spring Street were out in our front yard. All the dogs were there, too.

When Sunday school was over, Rusty and Janet and I went all around town so that Rusty could show me off. Everyone told me what a smart and beautiful dog I was. The man who jumped out of bed on the wrong side had a good word for me today. Boy, was I a hero! There never was a dog like me.

Now, maybe you do not think
I was a hero.
I know I did not bark and bark
to let someone know
that his house was on fire.
I did not pull a little girl
out of the water just in time.
A little girl who could not swim!
I did not track down the bad men
who were out to get your money.
But I did learn
how to live in a city.
I did get my picture
on the front page of the paper.
Now, I ask you. Isn't that enough
to make me a hero? Isn't it?

Words

Words make me think of things.

When I say over,
I think of clover,
White clover growing
Where grass is green.

When I say why,
I think of the sky
And see white birds
As they fly by.

When I say hark,
I see the lark
Fly up from her nest
And sing to the sun.

When I say end,
I think of a friend.
When I say who,
I know it is you.

The Mystery at Shadow Lake

Picture Dictionary

light bulb

button

cabin

crow

Highway 66

key

leaves

station wagon

window

Words You Can Get by Yourself

cake	let	may	all
lake	pet	pay	fall
		pays	falling
space	move	and	know
place	prove	stand	known
		stands	
never	socks	hop	faster
ever	locks	pop	fast
forever	locked	popped	last
	unlock		
	unlocked		

luck	wind	good	hard
Lucky	Windy	goody	hardly
long	go	did not	end
longer	goes	didn't	send
it is	cannot	some how	for give
It's	can't	somehow	forgive
sun light	tumbling	any where	out doors
sunlight	tumble	anywhere	outdoors

Let the Sentences Help You

Where have you been?

I take good care of my books.

Will your dad let you drive the car?

drives driving driveway

My money is all gone.
I have nothing left.

I am too tired to walk any farther.

Will you open the door for me?

I will be one of the actors in the play.

actor

The sun will shine before long.

shining monkeyshines

The fire will burn for a long time.

burned   burned-out

Turn to the right at the next corner.

turned

The sun comes up early in the morning.

Dave is one of the boys in our gang.

Let the Sound Help You

Say the word too to yourself. Listen to the sound of oo. Now help yourself with these words.

spook	roof	swoop
spooky		swooped
spookier		

Let the Syllables Help You

mystery   mys′ter y   mysteries   mys′ter ies

Some Words Have More Than One Meaning

fall — 1. The time of year when leaves fall. 2. To tumble down.

leave — 1. To go away. I will leave home at noon. 2. To let stay. I will leave my dog at home.

Something Spooky

If you want to have fun,
find yourself a good mystery.
That is what we did this fall
when we were up at Shadow Lake.

Do you know what a mystery is?
A mystery is something spooky.
Surprising things start to happen,
one after another.
No one can find out why.
A mystery is a big, dark secret.
It is a question without an answer.

If you let a mystery
get its hands on you,
it will tease you and tease you.
You have to find out how it happened.
You are good for nothing
until you do find out.
By that time it is no longer a mystery.
The fun comes in working it out
and finding the answers.

Now are you ready for my story?
It will be a spooky one.
If I tell it well enough,
you may want to make it into a play
that you can put on at school.
So I will start out by telling
who the actors are going to be.

The Actors in the Play

I will be the first actor.
You know me. I am Rusty Wells.
I live in Redwood City
with my grandmother and grandfather.
Mother and Dad are away on a long trip.
When they come home
from across the sea,
they will live in our house with us.

Man! What school can do to a fellow!
If it had not been for school,
I could have gone on that trip, too.
Just think of what I missed.

The next actors will be the boys
in the Spring Street gang.
Don't get the idea we are a bad gang
that makes trouble for other people.
We are just a gang of boys who live
on Spring Street and play together.
We are not too goody-goody.
No boy wants to be a goody-goody.
But we hardly ever do anything wrong.
Hardly ever!
There are dads and mothers around
to keep an eye on us, and that helps.

You have known some of us
for a long, long time.
Me, Mark Waters, and David Lamb!
Then there are Windy Chase,
Buddy Barns, and Lucky Masters.
Just enough boys for Grandfather
to take in the station wagon
when he goes to Shadow Lake!
Shadow Lake is where the mystery
is going to happen. Don't forget that.

The next actor is my grandfather.
He and I are buddies.
He owns our house in Redwood City
and a cabin up at Shadow Lake.

When the fall days are over,
he puts everything away
and locks up the cabin.
It stays locked up until spring.

This fall we moved into a new house.
Grandfather had so much to do
that he forgot about the cabin.
He just happened to think of it
on the day this story starts.

This next actor does not live in Redwood City.
He is Mr. Shark, and he lives in a little town not too far from Shadow Lake.
He sold the cabin to Grandfather.
Grandfather lets him have a key.
Mr. Shark drives out every day or so to keep his eye on things when Grandfather is not around.
But this time Mr. Shark did not keep his eye on the key.
That is how the mystery started.

What you see in the picture
can't be an actor, as you well know.
But you have to know
what the cabin looks like,
where the mystery takes place.
So here it is.

The cabin is back in the woods.
There are no other cabins
anywhere around.
It is dark back there in the woods,
and spooky enough to start with.
It will get spookier as time goes on.

Are you wondering
what this question mark is all about?
It stands for the last actor.
You will not know who he is
until my story comes to an end.
I don't know how you can make
an actor out of him,
but he can't be left out.
He is the one to blame for the mystery.
He will have to get in somehow.

This puts an end to the actors.
Now it is time for the story.

The Grand Idea

It was a beautiful fall day when that grand idea popped into Grandfather's head.

Grandfather was out in our front yard. Red leaves were falling all around. He looked at the sun and the blue sky. He listened to the wind in the trees.

"Days like this can't last forever," he said to Grandmother. "I had better see about that cabin. I can't put it off any longer."

When I came home at noontime,
what do you think he said?

"How about going up to the lake
with me tomorrow? You and your gang!
We can go in the station wagon.
We can stay all night at the cabin
and come back home on Sunday."

How did I like that idea?
How did it suit the rest of the gang?
We were good for nothing in school
that afternoon.
It is a wonder we did not have to stay
after school for whispering
and for not doing our work.
But we got by somehow.

Janet and the rest of the girls
were going to the zoo
on Saturday afternoon.
When we told them the grand idea,
all they said was, "What do we care?"

Early the next morning
we were in the car all ready to go.
We were ready long before Red, my dog,
left for the post office.
You know all about Red and the postman
and how Red became a hero.

This morning Red wagged his tail
hard enough to make it fall off.
I hated to leave him at home,
but it was not my fault.
What could I do?
A gang of boys and a great big dog
in one station wagon
were just too much for Grandfather.
Red will never forgive me. I know that.

The station wagon whizzed along down the highway to the lake. Before too long the gang got tired of just looking. We started pulling at one another the way boys do.

"Cut out the monkeyshines," called Grandfather. Boy, was he cross! He was not going to stand for any nonsense when he was driving.

For a long time after that everything seemed to be going well. Then all at once Grandfather pulled off the highway and stopped the car.

"This can't be," said Grandfather.
"It just can't be!
Did I leave the key to the cabin
in my other coat pocket?"

Now what were we going to do?
Turn back to wait for another day?
Not if the gang had anything to say!

At last Grandfather found a way out.
"When we get to the next town,
I will call up Dave Shark.
He can drive out with his key."

So Grandfather put in the call.
The gang had hamburgers and ice cream.
Grandfather was so mad at himself
that he didn't want any lunch.

"Dave is on his way by now,"
said Grandfather, as the car started.
"He will leave the key
in a safe place under the back step."

We got to Shadow Lake
in the early afternoon.
It was a beautiful fall day.
The lake was as blue as could be.
The sun was shining all around.
It was not dark in the woods today.

I was the first one out of the car.
I ran ahead to get the key.
Right then the mystery started.
There was no key under the step.

I Don't Like the Looks of Things

We poked around and poked around under that step. No key!

So Grandfather turned the car around. He stopped at a farm on the highway to put in another call for Dave.

What did Mr. Shark have to say?

"That key is TOO there. Right under your nose! Anyone with two eyes in his head could not help seeing it."

"Well, now," said Grandfather. "We can't find it with 14 eyes."

"I'm on my way out to prove it to you," said Dave.

So out he came, but he didn't prove a thing. The key was not there.

"Upon my word, I put it there,"
said Dave, over and over again.
"Someone ran away with it.
Who wants a key to this cabin?
If you ask me, I don't like
the looks of things around here."

Right there and then
we all started to feel spooky.
The mystery was after us.

The two men worked away at a window
until they had it open.
Then I climbed in
and unlocked the front door.

After that we boys made for the lake. The men stayed in the cabin.

The sun was going down. Outdoors it was not too warm. We saw a fish jump up from the water. Dave had told us that there was a red fox in the woods by the lake, but we did not see him. All the animals we saw were squirrels. They ran around, as bold as could be, looking for acorns. Not one frog or turtle did we see.

"They are down in the lake, asleep in the mud," said Lucky. "They will stay there until spring."

When we came back to the cabin,
Mr. Shark was on the back steps,
ready to leave for home.

"Hi, there! Get a move on!"
he called, when he saw us.
"And by the way! Tell me what you did
with my car keys.
I left them here on the step
when I looked for that house key."

"Yes, you did," said Windy and Mark.
"We saw you do it."

"So did we," said all the rest
of the gang, and Grandfather, too.

Where were the car keys now?

I can't tell you how hard and long we looked. No car keys anywhere! By this time things were getting spookier and spookier. It was a good thing that Mr. Shark had some other keys in the side pocket of his old car.

Grandfather had had no lunch. So after Mr. Shark had gone, Grandfather wanted to drive to town to get something to eat.

"We will leave a light," he said. "Anyone going by will know that there is someone at home here. Too bad there will be no moon! It will be dark here when we get back."

Was Grandfather feeling spooky, too? Maybe! What do you think? Anyway, we turned on a light and started off for town.

Lights Out

We were back at the lake again
before too long.
When we turned off the highway,
we looked for the light in the cabin.
There was no light anywhere.
We went on farther. Still no light!

When we came to the driveway
up to the cabin,
Grandfather stopped the car and said,
"You boys stay here in the car.
I will go into the cabin to see
what happened to that light."

Talk about being spooky!

"We had better get out of here and get out fast," said Lucky. "How about it, fellows?"

How could we get out? We could not drive the car. Anyway there was nothing to be afraid of. Every light in the place was on, and Grandfather was shouting, "Nothing wrong around here! Just a burned-out bulb!"

When we were ready for bed, Grandfather said, "Now see here! You fellows forget about those keys. Forget about that burned-out bulb. You are just as safe here as you could be at home. So go to sleep. No monkeyshines!"

So we did as we were told.

Once in the night I sat up in bed. What do you think I saw? Grandfather had moved his bed right across the back door. What do you know about that?

Mystery and No Mystery

Before we had time to eat
on Sunday morning,
Mr. Shark was back at the cabin.
He had a new lock for the back door.

"If someone gets in here,
it will not be my fault," he said.

Soon after that we left the men
to their work and made for the lake.
It was warm out in the sun.
So we left our sweaters in the cabin.

As we came out the door,
Mark saw something shining
on the ground by a tree.
Maybe you think he saw the lost keys.
The joke is on you. He didn't.
It was just a button off my sweater.
The sunlight on it made it shine.

"Put it on the step," I said.
"I will get it when I come back."

We stayed down by the lake
until the men called to tell us
that it was time to start for home.

We ran back into the cabin
to get our things together.
When I put on my sweater,
I happened to think about the button.
I went to get it, and then what?
Before I was out the door,
a big black crow swooped down
and flew away with it,
right under my nose.

"Cut it out, YOU!" I shouted.

By that time the old black crow was flying off into the woods. I turned around, and there were the men and the rest of the gang.

I don't know how long it was before we started to catch on. Mr. Shark was the first one to tumble. This is what he said.

"So it was that old black crow. Why didn't I know enough not to make a pet out of him? Every time I came out to the cabin, we had lunch together. This is the way he pays me back. Running off with my keys! Well, those keys are gone forever."

Now that is where Mr. Shark
was as wrong as he could be.

We all went outside to look around
for that old black crow.
This time we looked up, not down.
There on the edge of the roof
we saw them, shining in the sun.
Two car keys and a house key, too!
We never did find that button.

So this mystery turned out
just the way all mysteries do.
When you find the right answers,
there is nothing spooky about them.
But there is still one question
that I cannot answer.
How are you going to make an actor
out of that old black crow?

It's Fall

It's fall
When leaves come tumbling down
To cover the ground with red and brown.
It's fall
When fires send sparks to the sky,
And ducks in a V go flying by.

Captain Sam

Picture Dictionary

bus

fingers

letter

letter

presents

tickets

Words You Can Get by Yourself

can	as	did	am	big
fan	has	kid	Sam	bigger

in	in	stick
win	grin	kick
winning	grinned	side-kick
	grinning	

some where	out come	step	highway
somewhere	outcome	stepped	high
			high-school

and over	stand still	out stand
Andover	standstill	outstanding

walk away	fall	grow	legs
walkaway	fallen	grown	long-legged

Let the Sentences Help You

You see wild animals in the zoo.

wilder

I am captain of the football team.

cap′tain

We play football on a football field.

The team that wins is the champion team.

cham′pi on

Today I made a touchdown.

touch′down′

Then I kicked goal.

The score was 7-0.

scored scoring

I was the only player to make a score.

on′ly play′er

Let the Syllables Help You

November No vem′ber

Some Words Have More Than One Meaning

fan 1. Something used to move air to cool one off. 2. Someone who likes a game.

pop 1. A drink. 2. To jump up suddenly.

wild 1. Not tame, as a wild animal. 2. To act in a wild way.

Side-Kick

Mr. Lamb put his key into the lock, opened the car door, and stepped in. It was early morning, and he was on his way to work.

"By the way, Dave," called Mrs. Lamb from the open window. "Stop and get some light bulbs on your way home."

Just then someone or something popped out from somewhere and ran around the corner of the house.

"What goes on here?" asked Mr. Lamb.
"Oh, nothing," laughed Mrs. Lamb.
She turned to look at a boy
flying around the corner.
"This has been going on for days.
I told you about it last night.
Time was when I could not pull him
out of bed in the morning.
Now he is up and off
long before it is time for school.
No mystery about this!
He has found himself a hero,
and you know who."
"A hero works wonders,"
said Mr. Lamb with a big grin,
as the car started down the drive.
By this time young Dave
was around the corner on Gates Street.
He turned left again at Lake Street.
Then he stopped at a big white house.

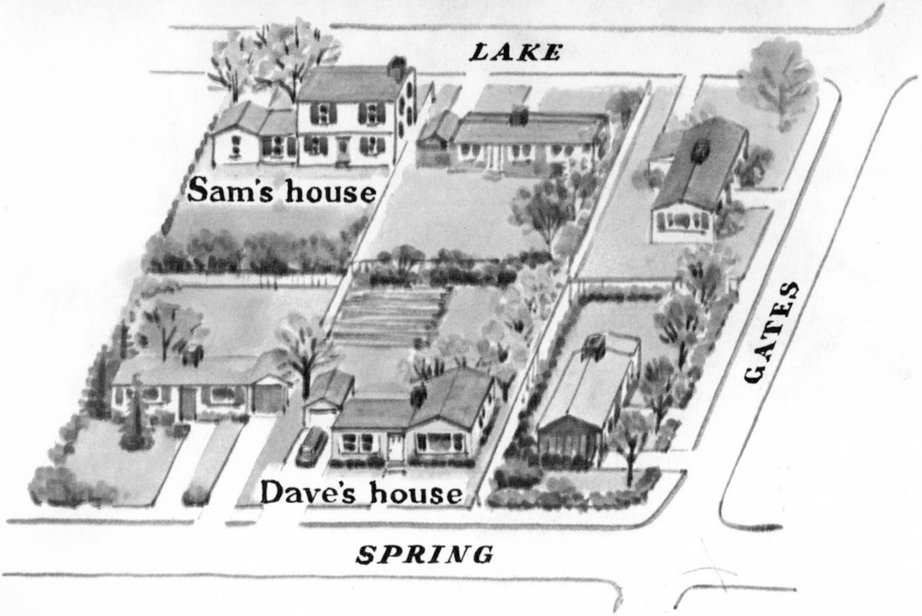

Why had Dave come here on the run? He stopped long enough to take out a dime and a nickel from his pocket. For some time all he did was stand around, kicking up leaves. There was nothing here for him to do. He was waiting for someone. Anyone with any imagination could tell that.

Before too long Sam Burns, a big, long-legged high-school boy, came down the driveway.

"Hi, there! Are you here again?" said Sam, handing over his books and grinning down at Dave. "Don't you ever stay at home?"

"Hardly ever," answered Dave, grinning right back at him. "How is the team coming by now?"

"Well, if you ask the captain, not well at all," answered Sam. "We will have to work our heads off to win that game on Saturday."

"Go ahead and work then," said Dave.
Anyone looking at him now could see that he was feeling great. Who could blame him? Here he was, walking to the bus stop with the captain of the Redwood City football team. Here he was, talking over the game just as if he were one of the team. Boy! Was this something! What did he care if the fellows at the bus stop poked fun at him?

"Hi, Sam! Who is your side-kick?" they called, grinning at one another. "Are you going to put him on the team?"

Maybe Dave was Sam's side-kick. What did he care? Being side-kick to a football captain was all right with him.

He stayed until the last fellow to climb on the bus called, "So long, kid!" Then he made his way back home. He sat on the steps at Mark's house to wait until Mark was ready for school.

"Boy, but Mark is a slowpoke," he said, as he pulled up his socks. "He will never make a football player."

The Big 10

Saturday came, and Redwood High did win the game.

All the football fans in town shouted their heads off.

"We told you this was our year," they said to the fellows on the team. "Here we are, off to a good start. Keep up the good work, and anything can happen. You may turn out to be the best team in the Big 10."

The Big 10 were the football teams from the 10 big high schools in and around Redwood City. The Redwood team was one of them.

That Saturday the game had been at Andover, not at Redwood High. So Dave did not go. But he did follow the game on TV, and he read all about it in the Sunday paper.

"How come?" he said to Sam on the next trip to the bus stop. "You didn't win by much. 13 to 12! What was wrong with you?"

"Wrong with us?" said Sam.
"What are you talking about?
Those Andover Colts have a good team.
A better team than we have!
We were lucky to win at all."

"Then how come you are going to be the champions of the Big 10?
Just tell me that," Dave went on.

"CHAMPIONS!" said Captain Sam.
"Where did you get that idea?
Who said anything like that?"

He went on standing where he was, too surprised to say another word.

"YOU did! Yes, you did!" said Dave. "You said so to the other fellows. You said, 'Boy, if we only could!'"

"Maybe I did, but I was only talking. So were the other fellows," said Sam. "Don't let that talk go any farther. We can't start to crow after just one game. It never pays to talk big. So you keep still. Do you hear?"

"All right, I will," said Dave. "But you had better be the champions. Better find yourself a four-leaf clover."

Not a Walkaway

It was hard to keep from crowing
in the days that followed.
Redwood High went right on winning,
one game after another.
Sometimes the team played out of town.
Sometimes it played
on its own football field.
Sometimes it played other teams
that were not in the Big 10.
But all the time Sam and his team
went right on winning.

Everyone in Redwood High
had gone wild over the team.
Every Saturday afternoon,
when the football game was in town,
the fans were out at the field.
They were shouting their heads off.

Those high-school fans
were not the only wild actors.
The grown-up fans were just as bad.

"We will make it this year," they said.
"This will be the first champion team
Redwood City has ever turned out."

Saturday after Saturday went by.
There was just one game left to play
in the Big 10.

Where was the game to be?
On the Redwood City football field!
What teams were to play?
Redwood High and the team
from the Great Falls High School!
When was the game to be?
On the last Saturday in November!

Could Redwood High win the game?
That was the burning question.
Redwood had an outstanding team.
There was no question about that.
But the fellows from Great Falls
were much bigger.

There were some people wise enough
to say over and over again,
"Don't start crowing too soon.
Great Falls may prove to be
the bigger and better team.
This game is not going to be
a walkaway for one team or the other."

Red-Letter Day

Now all there was left
for Sam and his team to do
was to win that game.
If they could do that,
the last Saturday in November
was going to be a red-letter day
for their home town.

For David Lamb,
it was going to be a red-letter day
in two different ways.
It was the day of the game
and his birthday at the same time.

"What do you know?" he said,
when he first found this out.
"What do you know about that?"

When Dave got over his surprise, he turned to his dad and mother.

"I don't want a party," he said. "I don't want a birthday cake. Hot dogs and pop out at the field are better than any old cake. All I want for my birthday is to see Sam win that game."

"So you don't want a party. You don't want a cake," said his dad. "You don't want any birthday presents."

He didn't smile as he said this. So David knew he was not joking.

"Oh, come on, Dad," said Dave.
"Could you do that to me? Could you?
I didn't say a word about presents."

"But I did," said his dad.
"That is the way it will have to be."

Dave looked anything but happy.
His dad went on looking at him
out of the corner of his eye.

At last Dave looked up and said,
"All right, Dad. I give in.
No presents!
I just have to go to that game."

Then Mr. Lamb went on to say,
"This is what I will do, Dave.
Mr. Wells and I will drive
to the field in his station wagon.
I will see about getting tickets
for us and for you and your gang.
I will take you all to the game,
and that will be your birthday present.
But there will be nothing else
from Mother and me. Not one thing!
How about it?"

"How about it? It's keen!
Just keen!" shouted Dave.
"Anyway, Grandmother and Grandfather
will send me something.
Uncle Will will, too.
May I tell the gang now? I can't wait."

Then off he flew.

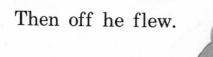

Who were the boys David asked to the game? You know. They were the same boys who went on that spooky trip to the cabin at Shadow Lake. The same boys who saw Mr. Shark's pet, that old black crow! The crow that swooped down and flew away with Rusty's button! The one that put the keys on the roof!

When Dave told his good news, that Spring Street gang went wild. Wilder than all the grown-up fans and the high-school fans put together!

Keep Your Fingers Crossed

"It's my birthday tomorrow,"
said Dave to Sam
on the day before the game.
"So win that game, old boy!"

"What if I don't win?" grinned Sam.
"Will you still be my buddy?"

"I don't know about that. Maybe!
But don't count on it," said Dave.

"Anyway, I will do my best,"
said Sam, as he climbed into the bus.
"So long, side-kick!
Keep your fingers crossed!"

The last Saturday in November turned out to be a beautiful day. Fall was about over, and it was not warm out at the field. But the sun was shining, and the field was dry. Just the way the two teams wanted the field to be!

No one had any trouble keeping warm. How could he have trouble when he was jumping up and down and shouting for his home team?

Not all the fans were at the game.
Some of them could not get tickets.
So they sat at home and looked at TV.

Everyone was on edge,
waiting for the game to start.

The boys in the Spring Street gang
could not keep still.
As soon as they sat down,
they jumped right up again.

"By the way, fellows," said Mr. Lamb.
"Here is one thing I forgot to say.
I don't want to hear a peep out of you
if Great Falls wins the game.
Not one peep! Do you hear?
If you can't take it,
turn around and go home right now."

"We know, Dad," answered Dave.
"But Sam IS going to win.
I have my fingers crossed.
All the other kids have, too."

It was a good game
right from the start.
Two good teams were playing
as they had never played before.

Maybe the crossed fingers
of the Spring Street gang did some good.
Long before the first quarter was over,
a player from Redwood High
made a touchdown. Then he kicked goal.

Redwood High 7   Great Falls 0

The Redwood fans went wild,
and the Spring Street gang
went right along with them.

"See, Dad! I told you so,"
shouted Dave.
"Now what have you to say for yourself?
Now who has the better team?
Now who will be the champions?"

"It looks like our side,
but don't crow too soon," said his dad.
"There are still three quarters to go,
and anything may happen."

But nothing did happen.
The game seemed to be at a standstill.
The next two quarters went by.
No one scored a touchdown,
so no one could kick goal.
The score still read

Redwood High 7 Great Falls 0

Now it was the last quarter,
and time was running out.
Could Redwood High
keep Great Falls from scoring?
If they could, they were the champions.

Some Redwood fans started to shout,
"It's all over! The game is ours!"

Maybe it was crowing too soon
that did it. Anyway, something did.
All at once the Great Falls team
was off down the field.
Then, in front of everyone's eyes,
their captain scored a touchdown.

And then . . . .

With every fan at the game
waiting for the outcome,
that same captain kicked goal.

This was it. The big game was over.

Redwood High 7 Great Falls 7

The Redwood fans looked as if
the sky had fallen on their heads.
So did the Spring Street gang.

It was a good thing
Mr. Lamb was there to keep saying,
"Not a peep out of you. Don't forget!
It was only a football game,
and nothing to cry about."

"Yes, but Dad," said Dave,
when he could stand it no longer.
"Who are going to be the champions?"

"We may not have a champion team," answered Mr. Lamb. "Not this year! But we have one of the two best teams in the Big 10. Isn't that enough?"

When Dave got home, there were presents from Uncle Will and from Grandfather and Grandmother. They helped him to feel a little better and forget about the game.

On the morning of the next school day he was back in the same old place in front of the house on Lake Street.

"Hi, there! So my side-kick didn't go back on me, after all," said Sam, grinning down at him.

"What do you think I am?" asked Dave, grinning back at him. "I didn't, and I never will."

How Any Fellow Feels

My Sunday suit is a good-looking suit,
But somehow I don't like it.
I don't care what my mother thinks,
I could get along without it.

But football suits and swim suits,
And suits like that, you see,
Those are the suits a fellow likes,
And those suits just suit me.

A Dad Who Remembered

Picture Dictionary

face

kitchen

rain puddle

robe

shovel

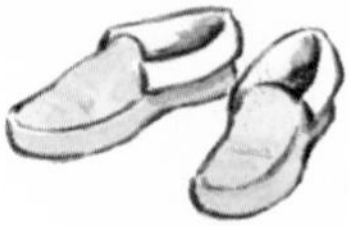
slippers

Words You Can Get by Yourself

old	door	book	gate	hops
cold	floor	took	late	tops

team	smile	bed	all ways
dream	while	sled	always

run	make	catch	branch
runners	making	catches	branches

slow	help	happy	stop
slowly	helpful	unhappy	stopping

to night	softly	red	mad
tonight	soft	redder	madness

still	light	care
stiller	bright	careful
stillest	lightest	careless
stillness	brightest	

could	us	grow	well	hop
should	dust	throw	bell	flop
would	must	throwing	belly	

cake	actor	run	roof
wake	act	runt	goof
waked	acting	grunt	goofy

could not	fun	football	touchdown
couldn't	funny	foot	touch

over time	bed room	side walk
overtime	bedroom	sidewalk

show	lakes	snowball	snowflakes
snow	flakes	snowfall	snowman

play ground	news paper	oi	oi
playground	newspaper	join	noise
		joined	noises

Let the Sentences Help You

I eat breakfast in the morning.

My work is all done.

There are 7 days in a week.

See that your hands are clean
before you eat.

One and one are two.
That answer is not hard. It is easy.
When I feel afraid, I feel uneasy.

I will use my key to unlock the door.
used

Mark gave me a game for my birthday.

Let the Syllables Help You

member	mem′ber	winter	win′ter
remember	re mem′ber	middle	mid′dle
remembered	re mem′bered	dinner	din′ner

One Winter Night

Windy Chase turned over in bed and opened his eyes. His head and all the rest of him were away down under the covers. It was warm and dark down there. He could not see a thing.

Windy pulled back one corner of the covers and peeped out. It was cold out there. He could feel it on his nose. The corner of the room he was looking into was as black as night.

NIGHT! That is what it was. The middle of the night! What made him feel that something was going on around here? Something different! What was wrong with him? No one had called him. It was not time to get up.

For a time he stayed where he was, just listening. It had never been so still before. No cars going by on Spring Street! No wind to move the branches of the tree outside his window! No dogs barking! Not one of the little soft noises you hear in a house at night!

Just stillness! Too much stillness! That was what was wrong. Windy kicked back the covers and sat up in bed. Then he knew. Oh, boy, did he know! He jumped out of bed and made for the window.

Great flakes of snow were coming softly down out of the night sky. The trees and roofs were covered with white. Great white flakes had turned the yard, the driveway, and the street into one great white field.

The first snowfall of the winter! That was what this was, and here he was at the window.

No wonder he had waked up. Just think of it. He was the only one in this house who knew what was going on. The only kid on Spring Street, too! Boy, was this something! Just think of the fun he could have tomorrow.

Yes, but where was his sled? Out in the garage in back of 50 other things! He had asked his dad to get it out.

"Time enough for that," his dad had said. "It never snows in November."

Now see what had happened. His dad was not so smart, after all.

Man, it was cold around here. Windy turned to put on his robe and slippers. Right there and then he had a wild idea. Why didn't he put it out of his head and go back to bed? Not Windy!

He was going to get that sled out and get it out now. No waiting around until tomorrow morning! Nothing wrong about that! Just so he didn't wake up his mother and dad!

He opened the door of his room and stepped out. He was as still as a boy could be in the middle of the night.

Wild and Wilder

Slowly, softly, step by step, Windy started for the kitchen. There was a door from there down into the garage.

Now his head was working overtime. Be careful when you turn the key. Be careful when you step down into the garage. Careful when you shut the door! O.K. Turn on the light! Safe at last!

Don't start to pull that sled out from under the things in front of it. Move one thing and then another. And, man, don't make any noise!

Once Windy did make some noise. Then all he could do was stand still to see what happened. Luck was with him. Nothing happened! Not one thing!

At last there was his sled over by the side door all ready for morning. There was Windy, all covered with dust.

One wild idea was enough for one night. Why did Windy have to have another idea, wilder than the first?

Could he? Oh, boy, could he? Just one belly flop down the driveway? There was no one going by in the street at this time of night.

Was there anything wrong with that idea? Yes, there was, and you know it. You take time to think before you act. It is too bad that Windy was not like you. He did the first thing that came into his head, without thinking. That is why he got into trouble. Out the side door he went, and around the corner of the garage.

Man, it was cold outside. The snow came down on Windy and up over the tops of his slippers.

Now he was standing in front of the big garage door with his sled up in front of him. One good run down the driveway! Down came the sled. Down landed Windy with a good belly flop on top of it. Down, down went the sled, across the street and up the drive on the other side.

Boy, was this something to tell the gang about! Windy grinned away to himself, a great big grin. How still everything was. No one around to see what he was doing and to tell him not to! No one going by in the street! Oh, boy, what fun!

Then all at once, when it was too late, he started to think. Boy, would he catch it when his dad and mother found out! Boy, would he catch it tomorrow morning! They would take away his sled, too, and not give it back for the rest of the winter. That is what they would do. Man, was he in trouble!

Just thinking about what would happen made Windy forget to put things back where they belonged in the garage. Anyway his fingers were too cold. He forgot to lock the door into the kitchen. He just left his sled by the side door of the garage and made for bed. If he had been still before, he was stiller now. He popped back into bed and covered his head.

Outside the window the snowflakes came softly down out of the night sky. Inside the room his robe and slippers made puddles of water on the bedroom floor. Down under the covers an unhappy blue-eyed boy was saying to himself,

"Oh, boy! TOMORROW!"

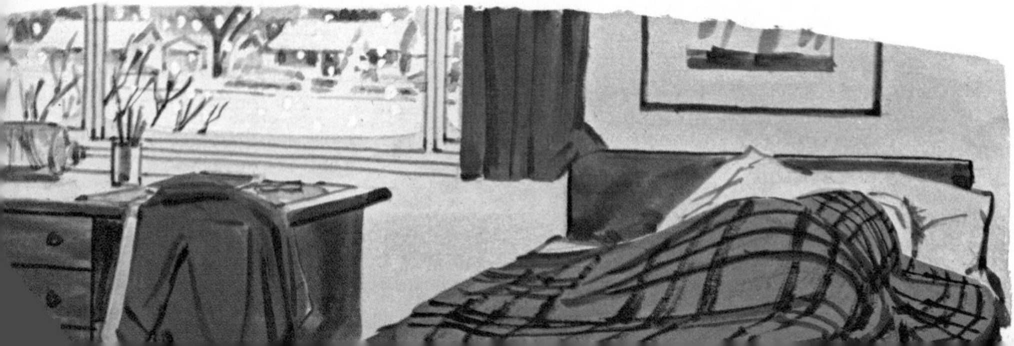

Oh, No! It Couldn't Be!

"Windy, wake up! Come on, boy! Get a move on you. Just look out the window."

Mr. Chase poked his head in at the door of Windy's room and waited for an answer. All he could hear was a grunt from down under the covers.

"Open your eyes, boy! It's snowing outside. Did you hear me?"

Still only a grunt from Windy.

"All right then! Stay where you are," said his dad, turning around and walking back the way he had come.

"Kids are different today. What is wrong with them?" asked Mr. Chase. He was talking to Windy's mother, who was getting breakfast in the kitchen.

"They don't get a kick out of anything," Mr. Chase went on. "When I was a boy, nothing could have made me stay in bed on a morning like this. I would have been out with my sled before breakfast. Not Windy! I can't get him out of that bed long enough to take one good look out the window. Sometimes I am about ready to give up."

"Don't do that," said Windy's mother.

Mr. Chase walked to the kitchen window to look out at the snow. The white flakes were still coming down. As he was standing there, he started to smile. His smile turned into a grin. His grin ended in a big laugh.

"What is so funny?" asked Mrs. Chase.

"Oh, nothing!" he answered. "I was just thinking of something I did once when I was a boy. Man, did I catch it from my dad. I was a champion when it came to getting into trouble. Remember to ask me to tell you about it. It will be just as well if Windy never finds out what happened. Now I had better shovel the drive and back out the car."

He walked over to the door into the garage. He started to turn the key the right way to unlock the door. The key did not turn. The door was not locked.

"Well, of all things," said Mr. Chase to himself, as he stepped down into the garage. "I forgot to lock this door last night. How careless can I get?"

He looked around for the snow shovel. He saw it all right. It was right under his nose. The shovel was one of the things Windy had moved last night. Mr. Chase saw the other things, too. Little by little, the look of surprise on his face was growing bigger and bigger. In the end, his face looked like one big question mark.

What had been going on around here last night? Who had been in here, and what was he after? Not the car! It was still here. Nothing wrong with it!

Mr. Chase walked around to the other side to look the car over. It was then that his eye lighted upon something over by the side door. It was then that he saw IT.

It couldn't be. He must be seeing things. It just couldn't be. BUT IT WAS! There by the door was a sled, and under the two runners was a puddle of water.

All Mr. Chase could do now was to stand still, look at that sled, and get mad.

"What is this all about?" he seemed to be saying. "When did all this happen? Was it in the middle of the night? If so, that young man will hear from me. No wonder he stayed in bed."

Mr. Chase was as mad as a dad can be. Then he remembered what he had said in the kitchen. He remembered a long-ago night and another boy with a new sled for a present. Another boy just like Windy! He took the shovel and went out to shovel the driveway.

All the time he was shoveling, he was thinking things over. Anyone looking at him could tell that. He no longer looked so mad. All the madness was going out of him into the shovel. There was a little smile on his face, as if he knew a good joke that he was going to play on someone.

Without stopping to shovel the rest of the drive, he went back to the kitchen door.

"Come out here, Mary," he called to Mrs. Chase. "I have something to show you. See what you make out of this."

I do not know what happened to that breakfast. I only know that Mr. and Mrs. Chase went on standing in front of that sled for some time, talking.

Mrs. Chase ended up by saying, "All right, Sam. You win. Have it your own way. I just can't think that Windy would do a thing like that. If he did, he should have a good talking to and something else besides. But I will not let on. I will not say a word. Just remember this. If he catches a cold out of this, the two of you will hear from me. Don't forget that!"

What Goes on Here?

"Windy Chase, get out of that bed," called his mother from the doorway. "Do you want to be late for . . . ?"

Right in the middle of what she was saying, Mrs. Chase stopped talking. Windy peeped out from under the covers to see why. Her eye was on a puddle of water on the bedroom floor. Now he was in for it. Oh, boy, was he!

Mrs. Chase waited for a while. Then she said, "Young man, did you hear me?"

After that she just walked away.

This was funny. Windy took time to clean up the floor. All the time, he was saying to himself, "What goes on around here? She did call me young man, but why didn't she jump on me about this puddle?" He was as uneasy as a rabbit in a hole with a dog outside.

"Has Dad gone to work?" he asked, when he walked into the kitchen.

"Long ago," answered his mother, and that was all. She did not say a word about the snow. Not a word about the puddle! How much did she know anyway?

When Windy was ready for school, he opened the door into the garage. Now what? Everything he had put out of place last night was back in place this morning. There was his sled, too, back where it once was under 50 other things in the corner.

Had he had a bad dream? Was that what was wrong? Oh, no! A bad dream had not put that puddle on his bedroom floor.

Windy ran down the drive and all the way to school. There was not a boy or girl around anywhere.

The rest of the Spring Street gang were going in at the door when they saw him coming.

"Where were you?" they all shouted. "Boy, did you miss out on the fun! See that snowman out there on the playground. A fellow who rides the school bus helped us to make it."

When his room came out on the playground again in the middle of the morning, Windy helped to make snowballs to throw at the snowman. The boys had a place of their own on the playground with no girls around. So throwing snowballs here was all right.

Every once in a while Windy forgot what had happened and had a good time. Every once in a while he remembered last night. Then he was as uneasy as any boy is who has done something bad and is waiting to be found out.

"What is wrong with you?" asked Mark and David. "Don't you feel good?"

At noontime Windy's mother hardly said a word. Windy could remember the times when she gave him a good talking to. He didn't like those times at all. But why didn't she do that now? A good talking to was better than no talk at all. She knew about last night, and Windy knew that she knew.

After lunch he shoveled the rest of the drive. Why didn't his mother look out to see how helpful he was? When it was time for school, Windy was as uneasy as a bird when there is a cat around.

After school that night every boy on Spring Street ran home for his sled. So did Windy. He took one look at that sled away back under all those things in the garage. How about it? Maybe he had better not.

"I have to wait until my dad comes home," he said, as he joined the rest of the gang on the corner.

"Wait for your dad!" shouted Lucky. "Say, are you goofy? Can't you get that sled out by yourself? What is wrong with you? You have been acting goofy all day long."

"I'm not goofy!" shouted Windy. "If that is the way you feel, I'm going home. So there!"

So home he went and shoveled all the sidewalks. What did his mother say about that? Not one word!

How Come You Always Know?

What happened at dinner that night? Mother told Dad about the letter he forgot to take to the post office. She told about the tickets she had for a show Dad wanted to see. Dad told one or two things that went on at the office. No one asked Windy what went on at school. No one asked him how he liked the snow. No one asked him if he had fun. No one asked him a thing.

After dinner Dad put on his robe and slippers and sat down with the newspaper. Mother joined him in front of the fire. She went right on working on the puppets she was making for the school show.

Windy took out a book. It was a new book and a good one. It was called "How to Play Better Football." Windy was a football fan, just like David Lamb. All Windy wanted to do when he went to high school was to be captain of the football team. This book told all about keeping score. All about touchdowns and goal kicks and things like that! Tonight Windy did not care a thing about that book. He opened it and shut it again. He turned a page and then turned it back again. You know how uneasy a wild pony would be, locked up in a barn. That is how uneasy Windy was.

Time went by. At last Windy's dad put down his paper.

"By the way, Windy," he said, "how did you like that belly flop down the drive in the middle of the night? Or was it the middle of the night?"

Windy's head went down, down, down. It looked as if it would touch the floor. His face went on getting redder and redder. Then he started to cry. He didn't want to, but he did.

"Come on now. Start in and tell me all about it," said his dad.

It took a while for Windy to stop crying and get started. He knew that he was in for it all right. Once he did get started, just telling made him feel better.

"See here, young man," said his dad when the story ended. "I don't have to tell you what was wrong about what you did. You know what was wrong as well as I do. All I have to say is this. Don't ever let it happen again. Do you hear me? Now I have a story for you. You know that my birthday comes in November. Once when I was a boy, the only present I wanted was a sled."

Dad's story went on and on. Windy forgot his troubles and sat up to listen. Boy, what was this he was hearing?

Right in the middle of the story, Windy started to jump up and down. He would not let his dad go on.

"Dad, you didn't! You couldn't!" he shouted. "Don't tell me that you went out in the middle of the night!"

"I'm afraid I did," said his dad. "Do you know what happened to me? My dad used his slipper for something else besides putting it on his foot. That is just what I will do the next time I catch you going out in the night. Remember what I say, young man."

"Say, Dad," said Windy. "How come you always know when I do something bad, without anyone's telling you about it?"

"Oh, I was once a boy myself," laughed his dad. "Now off to bed with you. You have had a hard day. You are to come home from school and into the house every day for the rest of the week. You are not to touch that sled until I say you may. Don't forget, young man."

Things were bad, but not so bad as they could have been. Dad was right. It had been a hard day. Windy was as tired as any boy could be.

"Man, am I lucky to have a dad who remembered," he said to himself, as he pulled the covers over his head, shut his eyes, and went to sleep.

The Stillest Thing

Sunlight
Is the brightest.
Snowflakes on your face
Are lightest.
But the stillest thing I know
Is falling snow.

Mr. Alexander Wakefield Applegate

Picture Dictionary

angel

Christmas

marbles

pipe

whiskers

wings

Words You Can Get by Yourself

any	see	came	paint	clean
many	seen	name	painter	cleaners

bold	win	snow	sleep	give
bolder	winner	snowy	sleepy	giving

wake field	apple gate	wonder
Wakefield	Applegate	wonderful

have not	are not	spring is	winter is
haven't	aren't	spring's	winter's

tease	while	how ever	door step
please	pile	however	doorstep
pleased	piled		

earrings home made over coat

ears homemade overcoat

down hill poke pop no where

downhill poking popping nowhere

Let the Sentences Help You

Do you always have to be IT?
Give me a chance once in a while.

I will write the figure 9.

fig′ure

7 and 9 are 16. I figured that out.
Paint a figure of a man.

Not all my friends are boys,
but most of them are.

For the first time in my life,
I am going to fly across the sea.

Stop acting funny and pay attention.

at ten′tion

Let the Syllables Help You

Alexander

Al′ex an′der

order

or′der

ordered

important

im por′tant

suppose

sup pose′

supposed

The Winter of the Big Snow

Christmas had come and gone. The boys and girls on Spring Street had stopped dreaming about the presents they would get for Christmas.

Ahead of them was a long week of winter fun. No school to think about! Now they could skate on the homemade pond in Lucky's backyard. They could belly flop downhill on their sleds. They could do the many other things that made winter days so much fun.

This was a winter just made for boys and girls. The people in Redwood City had a name for it. They called it "the winter of the big snow."

The snow had started away back in November. Week after week it had gone on. Every snow shovel had been working overtime. Snow was piled high along the edges of walks and driveways.

"If it keeps on coming, where will we put it?" everyone asked. "Did you ever see a winter like this?"

A day or two after Christmas most of the Spring Street gang were hard at work, making still another snowman.

Down the street, with his hands in the pockets of his overcoat, came Mr. Alexander Wakefield Applegate. His face was red from the cold. His cap was pulled away down over his ears.

Mr. Alexander Wakefield Applegate was the most important man on Spring Street. Some people said that he was the most important man in Redwood City. He was a well-known painter. When he was not painting beautiful pictures, he was making beautiful figures of men and animals. People came from faraway places to see the beautiful things that he made. Mr. Alexander Wakefield Applegate was as important as his name.

The End of a Walk

Every morning, after breakfast, Mr. Alexander Wakefield Applegate had to go for a morning walk. That is why he was out on a morning as cold as this.

He was far too important to pay any attention to boys and girls. When one of them walked by him and said "Hi," he would always say "Hi" right back again. But that was all. He walked on with his head up as if there were no one around so important as he.

"He can't see me for dust," Mark used to say to the other boys. "All right for him. See if I care."

"Don't blame him too much," said Rusty's dad. "He is a great man. There are too many great ideas running around in his head. He can't see you or anyone else when he is thinking."

This morning there could not have been too many great ideas running around in Mr. Alexander Wakefield Applegate's head. When he saw the boys and girls at work on the snowman, he stopped. He looked over the top of the snow pile at the edge of the walk to see how they were getting on. Then he took some snow in his hands and started to make what looked like a . . . .

Was the great Alexander Wakefield Applegate going to make a snowball? Was he going to throw it, too?

No! That is not what he was doing. He seemed to be feeling the snow with his hands as if he wondered what he could do with it. He looked pleased with what he found out.

After a while he let the snow fall and turned around. He walked up the drive and across the yard to join the boys and girls.

What Is Wrong with You?

When Buddy Barns saw who was coming, he stopped work, with his eyes popping out. The others turned to see what he was looking at. Then they stopped, too.

MR. ALEXANDER WAKEFIELD APPLEGATE! What was he doing here? What did he want? What had they done wrong? Everyone looked surprised and uneasy. For a time, no one said anything. Red, Rusty's dog, gave a bark of surprise. One bark, and that was all!

You know as well as I do that dogs can always tell when there is a friend around. Red must have figured out that Mr. Alexander Wakefield Applegate was his friend. Anyway he ran over to him and wagged his tail like everything. Then what did the great man do? He gave a big grunt and patted Red on the head.

It may have been that pat that made Janet feel a little bolder. It made her bold enough to say, "Did you want something, Mr. Applegate?"

"Do I want something? I should say I do," said Mr. Alexander Wakefield Applegate. He went right on talking, as if he would never stop.

"What is wrong with you kids anyway? Is this the best you can do? I am so tired of snowmen that I never want to see another one in all my life. Haven't you any ideas in your heads? Haven't you any imagination?"

You may think that Mr. Alexander Wakefield Applegate was as cross as he was important. That is where you are wrong. While he was talking, he had tumbled over the snowman and had started to make something out of the snow. He looked pleased with himself and with everyone else. It was only the boys and girls looking at him who were too surprised for words.

Orders

For a while the only one working was Mr. Alexander Wakefield Applegate. The others, with their eyes popping out of their heads, were standing around him looking at something, but no one knew what. After a while the great man started to give orders.

"Go down to my house," he said to David. "Tell Mrs. Applegate that I want some of those things I use to clean my pipe."

Off ran David without an idea in his head as to what this was all about.

"One of you must have some marbles left over from last spring. Get me all you have," ordered the great man.

In at the kitchen door ran Lucky. Before long every kid was running home for one thing or another. Everyone who came back had someone else with him. Mr. Alexander Wakefield Applegate went right on working.

You should have been there to hear the noise and the chitter-chatter going on all around.

"Oh, boy, look at him now! Man, is he good! Cut it out. I had this place first. Is that what those pipe cleaners were for? Why couldn't we think up something like this? We must be goofy. Stop poking me. Boy, is he keen!"

By and by Mr. Alexander Wakefield Applegate got up off the ground.

"Out of the way, everyone," he said. "It's time to see how we came out."

Everyone stepped back to take a good look. There in the snow, and made out of snow herself, was the most wonderful cat you have ever seen.

Her whiskers were made out of pipe cleaners. The sun was shining on her green marble eyes, the brightest eyes a cat ever had. The end of her nose was a round black button. Her tail was long and beautiful.

That wonderful cat sat there in the middle of Lucky's front yard, looking just as important as Mr. Alexander Wakefield Applegate himself.

May the Best Man Win

When the boys and girls had had a good look at that wonderful cat, they tumbled all over one another. They forgot how important Mr. Alexander Wakefield Applegate was, and they tumbled all over him, too.

"Another one! Please!" they shouted.

"Not on your life!" said the great man. "But here is what I will do. Use your heads and your imaginations. I will give you until tomorrow afternoon. Prove what you can do on your own, and may the best man win."

"Win!" said Mark. "Win what?"

"I don't know myself," said Mr. Alexander Wakefield Applegate. "But by tomorrow noon I will. Be off with you now, and remember. NO CATS! May the best man win!"

When it was time for lunch, the Spring Street mothers had a sad time. Not one boy or girl wanted to come into the house. Not one wanted anything to eat. How could anyone eat when his head was popping with ideas?

"I will make an angel," said Ann. "A standing-up angel with wings!"

"A snow rabbit should be easy. Easy does it," said Windy.

"Wait until you see yourself made out of snow," said Rusty to Red.

"I have the winning idea," said Lucky. "I am going to make Uncle Sam."

So it went on. Those boys and girls had big ideas, all right. Their big ideas were working overtime.

Mark was the only one who did not say much. He went off by himself into the far corner of his backyard.

By the end of the afternoon, those big ideas were getting nowhere. Red did not think much of the dog Rusty made out of snow. So he tumbled it over. Ann's angel looked like a big old snowman. Her wings would not stay on. It was just as well that Uncle Sam was not around to see how he looked.

Most of the boys and girls were ready to give up, but they wanted to win, too. Maybe that is why they got together and walked down to Mr. Alexander Wakefield Applegate's house. All but Mark! He went on working.

When the great man came to the door, he saw about 100 kids on his doorstep.

"We aren't any good," Janet piped up. "And we want to win. Please come and help us a little. Please! Just a little!"

"Help you?" said the great man. "I am getting ready to go out to dinner. I have helped you all I am going to. Run along with you, and don't come back."

He looked down at the puddles of water all over the steps. Then he shut the door.

A Great Day for Spring Street

The next morning when Buddy Barns went out into the yard, there was Mr. Alexander Wakefield Applegate, looking at a pile of snow.

"What is this supposed to be?" asked the great man.

Buddy hated to tell, but he did.

"It's supposed to be a rocket," he answered. "I know it's no good."

Right then Mr. Alexander Wakefield Applegate started giving orders.

"Do this," he ordered. "Now this! Get a move on you, too."

At first he didn't touch the snow himself. Before long, however, he had to get his hands into it. He couldn't help himself. He wanted things to be right. Little by little the pile of snow started to look like a rocket.

"Now go on by yourself. I will be back after a while to see how you are getting along," said the great man. Then he walked on to the next yard.

All the rest of the day he had his work cut out for him. He went from one yard to the next. After he ordered those kids around and did much of the work himself, the angel's wings stayed where they belonged. The bear looked like a bear. Anyone would have known that it was Uncle Sam standing there as big as life in the snow.

By the end of the afternoon, cars were stopping all along Spring Street. People were getting out to see what was going on. No wonder they stopped. This is the way Spring Street looked in the late afternoon with the snowflakes falling all around.

The boys and girls were running around from one yard to another.

"See what we did! Aren't we good!" they went on saying, over and over again.

And the Winner Was — ?

Who was the winner? Was it Ann with her angel, Windy with his rabbit, or Rusty with his figure of Red? I am afraid you are in for a big surprise, and I will tell you why.

Mr. Alexander Wakefield Applegate was helping Janet to make a mother sheep with her lamb, when he saw Mark at work in the backyard. He walked over to see how Mark was getting along. He did not give any orders. He did not touch the snow. He did not say a word. He just looked and then walked away.

"He never did like me," Mark was thinking to himself. "He helps other kids, but not me. See if I care."

At the end of the afternoon, back came Mr. Alexander Wakefield Applegate. All the boys and girls were with him.

There on the snowy ground in front of Mark was a puppy asleep on the roof of a doghouse. The things Mark made were always good. So the little puppy and the doghouse were good. But they were not so good as Uncle Sam. Not so good as the big white bear! Not so good as the owl or the rocket! Then why did Mr. Alexander Wakefield Applegate look so pleased? Why did he say what he said next?

"Who made the rabbit?" he asked.

"I did!" shouted Windy. "Did I win?"

"Who made the rabbit?" asked the great man, looking Windy in the eye.

The rest of Windy's face that was not red from the cold turned red now.

"You made most of it," Windy said. "I couldn't do it by myself."

"Who made the owl?" That was the next question.

This time David knew the right answer.

"You did," he said. "I just helped a little."

So it went on from one boy or girl to another. The only one left was Mark. Then what did the great man do? He gave Mark a great big pat on the back.

"Good for you, young fellow," he said. "You didn't ask for help. You didn't get any. That makes you the winner."

Mark was too surprised to show how happy he was. It was only after the great man told him to come down the next day so that he could paint a picture of Mark and that sleepy puppy that Mark got over his surprise. His face was just one great big happy grin.

That night Mr. Alexander Wakefield Applegate sat down in front of the fire in his robe and slippers. As he put his newspaper on the floor, he said to Mrs. Applegate, "You know, Mary Ann. From the time this snow started, away back in November, I longed to get my hands into it to see what I could do. Those kids gave me my chance. I never knew that kids could be so much fun."

Spring's on the Way

I saw some tracks
On the snow-covered ground.
I followed them up to a tree.
There on a branch
On this cold winter day
A red bird was singing
As if it were May.

Can it be
That the red bird
Wanted to say,
"Winter's soon over.
Spring's on the way"?

Secrets Are for Keeping

Helping Yourself with New Words

Picture Dictionary

apple blossoms

basket

bees

For Mom and Dad
Because I love you
Princess Apple Blossom

cards

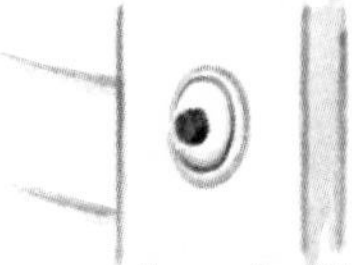

doorbell

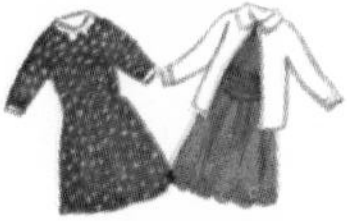

dresses

princess

table

tulips

Words You Can Get by Yourself

did	sing	think	hair	trip
hid	bring	pink	air	lip

pat	fish	turn	turn	give
Patty	Fisher	Turner	return	given

catch	skip	have	smile	take
catcher	skipped	having	smiling	taken

tease	chance	hill	forget
teasing	dance	sill	forgetful
	danced	silly	

slipper	be come	book	What is
slippery	become	cook	What's
		cooking	

who ever	Alexander	grass	grasses
whoever	Alex	pass	passes

see	weed	big	giggled
wee	need	gig	giggling
weed	needed	giggle	

Let the Sentences Help You

I call my mother Mom.
Let's ask our moms to take us to the show.
I hope they will say yes.

Do not help us.
We can do this by ourselves.

I will be ready in a minute.

I went to bed because I was so tired.
be cause′

The doorbell rang three times.

If you want me to hear you,
talk in a loud voice.

I like my friends, but I love my mom.
She loves me, too.

A beautiful thing is lovely.

My birthday comes in April.
A′pril

Make a list of things to get
at the store.

Don't forget to say "Thank you"
for your birthday presents.

Do you know what three and three are?
Of course I do.

Let the Sound Help You

Say the word JOIN. Listen for the sound oi. Use that sound to help you.

point appoint ap point′
disappoint dis′ap point′

---

dis′ap point′ed The way you feel when you do not get what you want.

New Names for Old

The long winter was over at last, and spring had come to Redwood City.

One warm spring afternoon Janet, Ann, Patty Fisher, and Mary Ann Turner were walking home from school together. They were chattering away to one another and giggling as girls always do when they get together. They were having a grand time just being silly.

Patty's house was their first stop on the way home. They always had a hard time saying good-by. So they sat down on Patty's front steps to take their time about it.

"Suppose you had another name," said Ann to Janet, with a big grin. "Suppose your name was Mrs. Long Nose. That is what I am going to call you. Mrs. Long Nose!"

"If you do, I will call you Mrs. Pickle Face," giggled Janet. "How will you like that?"

"Maybe you would like to be Mrs. Pop Eye or Mrs. Quack-Quack or Mrs. Slippery Snake," said Mary Ann.

"You had better not let the boys hear you," laughed Patty. "You know how boys are. Just give them a chance, and they will call you by those names forever. Anyway, they will until our moms put a stop to it."

"I know what we can do," Ann piped up. "We can think up some grand and important names, like Princess this or Lady that. We can call one another by our new names when no one is around. That can be our secret. I have my new name all ready. Lady Pigeon Wing! I saw that name in a book."

The other girls must have liked that idea. The next morning it was not Janet, Ann, Patty, and Mary Ann who walked to school together. It was Lady Green Slippers, Princess Snowflake, Lady Pigeon Wing, and Princess Apple Blossom. They walked along, looking up at the sky and feeling SO important.

Princess Apple Blossom

Lady Pigeon Wing

Lady Green Slippers

Princess Snowflake

I do hope that everything went well in school that morning. I would hate to think that Lady Pigeon Wing did not know what 7 times 9 was. I would hate to think that Princess Apple Blossom could not spell a little word like "angel" or "calf" or some bigger word like "whiskers" or "compass" or "attention."

What's Cooking?

That afternoon Rusty happened to see Patty as he came out of school.

"Hi, Pat!" he called. "How about playing ball? You can be catcher."

"I don't CARE to play ball," said Lady Green Slippers, looking up at the sky. "And I NEVER play with boys."

Rusty looked at her with his eyes popping out.

"What's cooking?" he asked. "Have you gone goofy or something?"

Patty did not answer. She just walked on, as if she did not see him.

It did not take the Spring Street gang long to figure out that something funny was going on, but they could not find out what it was. Boy, did that make them mad!

After dinner that night, Janet was helping Mother in the kitchen.

"Mom," she said in a whisper. "I have a secret to tell you. We girls made up some new names for ourselves. Just for fun, you know! My name is Princess Apple Blossom. Will you call me Princess from now on? Don't tell Mark, or he will tease the life out of me. Just call me Princess and don't say why."

Mom was so surprised at this news that she forgot to whisper back again.

"Princess Apple Blossom!" she said in a loud voice. "YOU, a princess? You don't always act like one."

Why did Mark have to show up right when Mom was talking? He laughed loud enough for the people next door to hear.

"So that is why you have been acting so goofy. Going around with your head in the sky! Wait until I tell the other fellows about this. Just wait!"

Then he went on making faces and saying in a little high voice, "How is Princess Apple Blossom today? MY, haven't we a beautiful name! MY, aren't we important!"

"See here, young man," said Mom. She did her best to look cross, but she was smiling to herself at the same time. "Janet is better than any princess I have read about. If she wants me to call her Princess, that is what I will do. So stop your teasing right this minute."

Before long Mom and the princess went into the other room where Mark and Daddy were looking at TV.

"Please, Princess, bring me Daddy's T-shirt," said Mother. "The one with the hole in it!"

"Princess!" said Daddy in a surprised voice. "That is a new name around here. It's a good one, too. I like it. While you are about it, Princess, will you bring me my pipe?"

Mark could tell by this that Mom and Dad were sticking up for Janet. He knew better than to say anything, but every once in a while he looked over at Janet and grinned. Then he poked out his lips as if he were going to say, "Pr . . . Ap . . . Bl . . . ."

Look at the picture on this page if you want to know how he did it. He poked out his lips, but not a word came out.

For the rest of the week, the girls had a bad time. How did the other boys find out about the secret? Of course, you know.

Every time the boys saw the girls coming, they grinned and poked out their lips. Mark showed them how. They followed the girls down the street with their noses high in the air. I hate to tell you what the girls did in return. They turned around and made faces at those boys all the way to school and back again.

What Day Is Tomorrow?

By the end of the week, the girls were tired of just going around with their heads in the air. So Patty said to the other three, "What did a lady or a princess do to have fun?"

"Oh, you know," said Mary Ann. "They put on beautiful dresses and white slippers and went to a ball every night. They danced and did things like that."

"Well, I'm not going to dance with any old boy," grunted Patty. "Couldn't they think up something better to do than that?"

The trouble was that the girls didn't know what a princess or a lady could do besides dance. It was then that Ann came up with a wise idea.

"Why not ask Miss Mary?" she said. "She knows everything, and she never tells. Not if you ask her not to!"

So off they ran to find Miss Mary.

It was a warm and beautiful morning. Miss Mary was pulling weeds in her backyard and singing softly as she worked.

Right in the middle of her yard was an old, old apple tree all covered with pink and white apple blossoms. The words she was singing went like this:

I know it is spring
When the sun shines bright
And apple blossoms
Are pink and white.

The ting-a-ling of the doorbell made Miss Mary stop her work. She walked around to the front door, and there she saw the girls. They sat down together on Miss Mary's front steps.

Miss Mary did not know that it was Princess Snowflake, Lady Pigeon Wing, Princess Apple Blossom, and Lady Green Slippers who had come to call on her, but she soon found out.

"So I'm to tell you what a princess would do on a beautiful spring day like this," she said.

A minute had not gone by before she had the answer.

"Well, now," said Miss Mary. "That didn't take me long. You couldn't have come to me for help on a better day. What day is today, anyway?"

"Saturday!" said all the girls in one loud voice.

"Nonsense!" said Miss Mary. "It is something else besides Saturday."

"Something else?" said the girls. They sat there wondering what the something else could be. Patty was the first one to tumble.

"The last day of April!" she shouted.

"Of course," answered Miss Mary. "And tomorrow will be . . . ."

All the girls knew the answer. I hope you do, too.

"What would a princess do for the ones she loves best on the first day of May?" Miss Mary went on.

The girls knew that answer, too. Do you? It's an easy one.

For the Ones We Like Best

Right after lunch the girls were back again at Miss Mary's house. In their hands they had most of the things they needed to work with. They piled all those things on the kitchen table.

Then they started in to work, with Miss Mary around to give the orders. The chitter-chatter around that table didn't stop for a minute all afternoon.

"Of course, we will all make a May basket for our moms and dads," said Ann. "But who else is going to get one?"

"Not those boys!" grunted Patty.

"Maybe I should make one for Red," said Janet. "I like him as well as anyone I know. If I put a hamburger inside, he will love that."

"How silly can you get?" asked Mary Ann. "A princess making a May basket for an old dog!"

"Don't forget Mr. Alex," said Patty.

At Christmas time, when Mr. Alexander Wakefield Applegate had made that wonderful cat with the green marble eyes, he and the boys and girls on Spring Street had become great friends. Now they all called him Mr. Alex because there was something friendly about that name and because it was easy to say. Of course, Patty was right. Mr. Alex just had to have a May basket.

"Maybe we should make a list," said Ann. "Janet, you are the best speller."

"Be careful! Don't put too many names on your list," said Miss Mary.

In the middle of the afternoon, while everyone was hard at work, Patty let out a great big OH.

"What are we going to put IN our baskets?" she asked. "We never said a word about that."

"Why should we?" asked Miss Mary, turning to look out her kitchen window. "Apple blossoms and May baskets just seem to belong together."

By the end of the afternoon, the May baskets were ready. How lovely they looked, side by side, on the table!

"They can stay there until tomorrow night just after dark," said Miss Mary. "Then we can put in the apple blossoms and start on our way."

"After dark? We can't!" shouted Ann. "We can't go out after dark."

"Let me take care of that," said Miss Mary. "Run along now. I have had a big day, and I am all tired out.

"What do you know about that?" said Miss Mary, as the girls ran down the walk. "All afternoon, and not one word about a May basket for me."

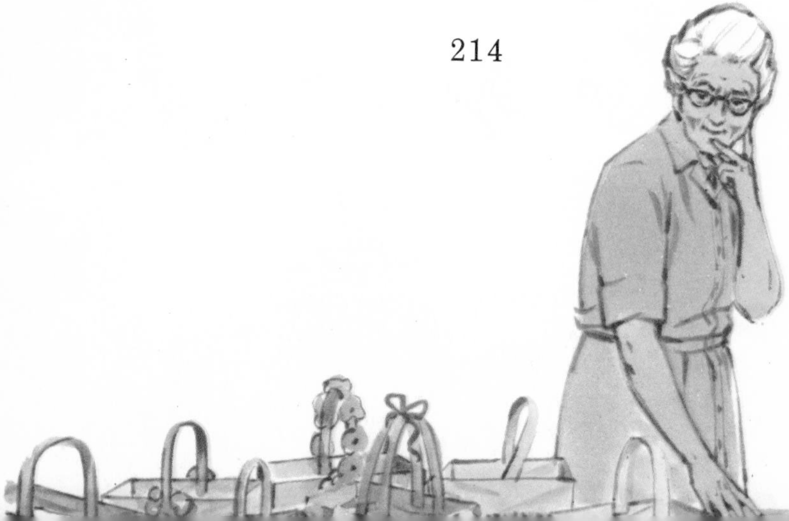

May Day at Last

It was a good thing that the next day was Sunday as well as May Day. Sunday school took up most of the morning. In the afternoon the girls went back to Miss Mary's house to write the cards to go on the baskets. This is the way one of the cards looked.

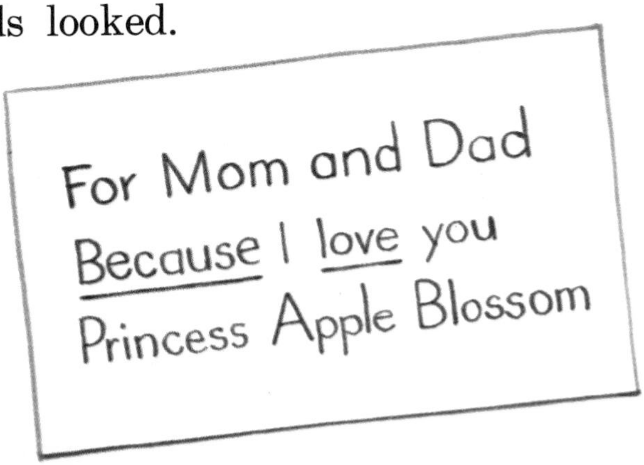
For Mom and Dad
Because I love you
Princess Apple Blossom

There was a card for every basket, but NO card and NO basket for Miss Mary. How could the girls be so forgetful?

The minute the cards were on the baskets, the girls ran for the door.

"We have to go," they said. "We have the most important thing of all still to do." They did not say what it was.

They ran down the street to Patty's house. There were no boys there to stick their noses in where they were not wanted. The girls worked at that important thing for a long, long time. They must have been pleased with it because their faces were all smiles. That important thing had to have a card, too. One big enough for every girl to write her name on it! Of course, you know what that important thing was.

"We can't put her OWN apple blossoms into her OWN basket," said Janet. "What are we going to do about that?"

Before long, four girls were standing outside the door of Mr. Alex's house, and Ann had her finger on the doorbell.

The minute the door was open, Patty said, "Mr. Alex, can you keep a secret?"

Then all the girls started talking at once, until Mr. Alex put his hands over his ears to keep out the chatter.

"Suppose YOU tell me what this is all about," he said, turning to Janet. "The rest of you KEEP STILL."

When I tell you that there were many beautiful tulips in Mr. Alex's yard, maybe you will know why the girls were there.

At first, when they told Mr. Alex what they were after, he said, "Not on your life! I am not pulling one of those tulips for anyone."

In the end, as always, he gave in.

"I suppose you can have some of them," he grunted. "Bring back that basket and let me put in the tulips. We may as well make it look like something."

"Thank you," called the girls, as they ran back down the walk. "We will bring the basket back with us. It can stay at your house until we need it."

Mr. Alex went back into the house.

"Do you know what I am?" he said to Mrs. Applegate. "An easy mark! A great big easy mark every time those kids come around. But after all, it's fun."

What is an easy mark? Do you know?

Because We Love You

Miss Mary had taken care of things, just as she had said she would. When the girls left for her house that night, their mothers said, "Stay as long as you like. Miss Mary will bring you home."

If you have ever made May baskets and taken them around to different houses, you know what happened after that. Miss Mary and three of the girls hid in back of some trees. The other girl skipped up to the door of a house, put down a May basket, rang the doorbell, and then scampered back to join the others.

Whoever it was who opened the door always looked surprised and pleased when he saw the basket. He always looked around to see who was giggling.

Mr. Alex called out in a loud voice, "I can't see you, but I know you are out there somewhere. Thanks for remembering an old man like me."

At last the baskets were all given out, and Miss Mary took the girls home. If she were disappointed, she did not let them know a thing about it.

"Well, now, that was fun," she said, as she unlocked her door. "I will listen to the news on TV and then go to bed."

She didn't have time to hear all the news. How could she? Her doorbell rang and rang and rang. There on her doorstep were four giggling girls. Ann's mother was with them. There on the same doorstep was the most beautiful May basket you have ever seen. The card on it said:

To Miss Mary
Because we love you
Princess Apple Blossom
Lady Green Slippers
Princess Snowflake
Lady Pigeon Wing

Spring

Spring brings
Many things.
Bees
And blossoming trees.
Birds calling.
Rain softly falling.
Warm days for playing.
A wind that keeps saying,
As it passes
Over the grasses,
"Let me whisper in your ear.
Spring's here."

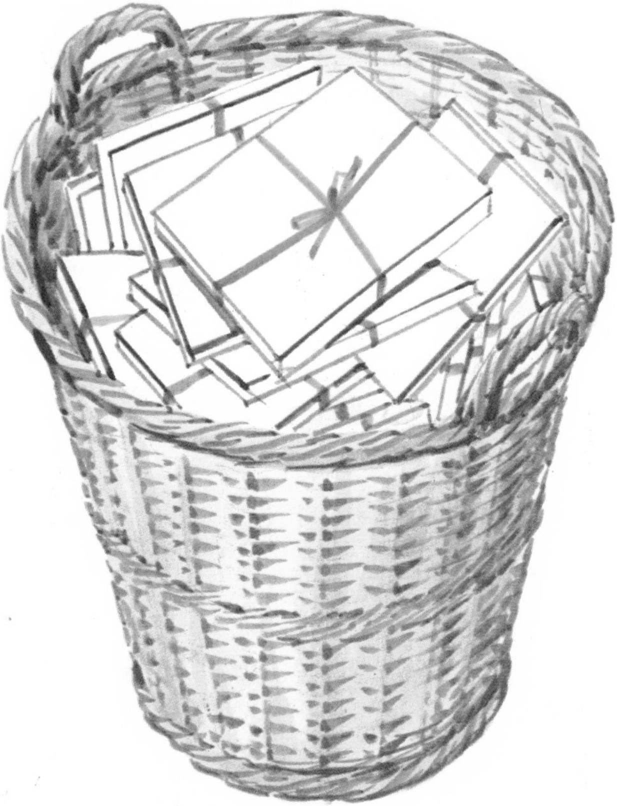

Too Much Is Too Much of Anything

Picture Dictionary

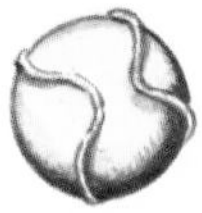

baseball

puzzle

Words You Can Get by Yourself

fox	take	hard	week
box	taking	harder	weekly
long	high	let	loud
longest	higher	letting	louder
walk	jump	wild	pile
Walker	jumpy	wildness	piling
will not	sun shine	swim	sad face
won't	sunshine	swimming	sad-faced
can	show	tired	stop
plan	low	tire	shop
plans	lowest	tiresome	shopping
ourselves	too	doorbell	day dream
themselves	boo	bell	daydream
yourselves	boost	most	daydreaming
	boosted	almost	

Let the Sentences Help You

When spring is over, summer comes.

sum′mer

We do not go to school in vacation time.

va ca′tion

Old things you throw away are called junk.

Do you agree with me?

a gree′ a greed′

If you fall, you may break your leg.

Then you will be sorry.

sor′ry sor′ri est

A broken leg is no fun.

Put 10 gallons of gas into my car.

From now on, I will buy gas at your station.

I hope my dog will win a prize at the show.

If you get dust in your eye, don't rub it.

I have lived here ever since I was born.

I entertained 10 boys at a cookout

in our backyard.

en′ter tain′ en′ter tained′

A Feeling in the Air

The bright spring days were almost over. April and May had come to an end. Apple blossoms and tulips were gone for another year, and summer was just around the corner.

Out in the Field School on Lake Street there was an uneasy feeling in the air. Everyone was waiting for something to happen. It was the last day of school. A little while, and it would all be over.

It was a hot afternoon, and Lucky Masters was daydreaming as he looked out the open window of Room 25. There was a smile on his face and a faraway look in his eyes. He did not hear the bee that came in with the sunshine and flew around his head. He was dreaming of baseball and swimming and bicycle rides and the trip he was going to take with his dad the day after tomorrow.

"Boy, will I have fun!" Lucky seemed to be saying. "This is the way to keep things cooking. Have your plans all ready. No waiting around for me!"

"Pay attention, Lucky," called Miss Walker from the front of the room. "Vacation isn't supposed to start until tomorrow."

She smiled when she said it, and Lucky grinned right back at her. He knew Miss Walker. She couldn't be cross on the last day of school. Maybe she was feeling jumpy, too. Maybe she couldn't wait for school to be over.

Just then a bell rang. It couldn't be. Yes, it was! School was letting out early.

Another two or three minutes, and boys and girls were piling out of every outside door, shouting louder than they had shouted since this time last year. Mr. Green, passing by on the street, parked his car to keep out of trouble.

"So long, gang!" shouted Lucky in a loud voice when he came to his own house. "I can play around with you tomorrow. After that, don't look for me. I won't be around for a while."

I Told You So

The next day was Saturday, the day when the Spring Street mothers did their weekly shopping. Today someone's mom stopped for Miss Mary. Then, one by one, the cars started off to be gone for most of the morning.

The Spring Street gang stayed at home. Shopping was tiresome. Boys and girls who had been in school for a year or two were supposed to be old enough to take care of themselves while their mothers were away. They WERE old enough, too, only today was different. Maybe it was because it was the first day of vacation, and they were still feeling wild.

The boys teased the girls, and the girls teased the boys right back again. They ran up and down the street from one yard to another. At last the girls hid in Miss Mary's backyard, where their silly giggling helped the boys to find them.

So here they were, boys and girls together, in Miss Mary's backyard. In front of them was that old apple tree.

It was a wonderful tree for climbing. The branches were low. One boost, and you could be up on the lowest branch. After that it was up to you. You could climb higher and higher on your own. Only you couldn't, and this is why.

"That is my tree, and you keep out of it," Miss Mary had told them again and again and again. "I am old enough myself, but that tree is three times as old as I am. Its branches may break at any minute. Someone may get a bad fall. Don't let me catch you climbing, or I will tell your mothers on you."

Well, Miss Mary couldn't catch them now. So how could she tell on them? When you have been longing to do something for a long time and the chance to do it is right under your nose, you know what happens. I hate to tell you that it was Janet who started all the trouble.

"Boost me up," she said to Buddy Barns. "Just to this first branch."

So Buddy boosted, and that was all that was needed. Before many minutes all the gang was up in the branches, making for the top of the tree. All but Ann! There was no one left on the ground to boost her. Anyway, she was afraid.

If any branch on that tree was going to break, it should have been the one Janet was standing on. She started the trouble. But things never work out that way. Lucky's name didn't help him. It was his branch that gave way, and down he came. Down, down on the hard ground!

I will not take time to tell you all that happened next. By the end of the morning Lucky was in bed with a broken leg. In bed, and you know where! The rest of the gang was at home, everyone in his own room. Everyone had had a good talking to from his mom and another one coming from his dad. Not one of them looked as if he could ever be happy again. The wildness was all gone out of everyone. And here it was, only the FIRST day of vacation.

Miss Mary was so mad that sparks seemed to fly right out of her eyes when she talked to Janet.

"I told you so! I told you so!" said Miss Mary. "And you a would-be princess! What's wrong with you? You seem to think that grown-up people don't know what they are talking about. Well, now you have found out. To think that you waited until I was not at home! Keep away from me. I don't want anything to do with you."

Miss Mary was so mad that she walked outdoors and started to pull weeds.

As for Lucky, what good were all his summer plans now?

"Too bad, my boy!" said his dad. "I must make that trip without you. I am just as disappointed as you are. Do as your mother tells you while I am gone."

Then he gave Lucky a good pat on the head and said good-by.

You could tell by Lucky's lips that he could hardly keep from crying. He was to blame for that broken leg, and he knew it. He was paying up for it, too. Anyway, his dad didn't rub it in.

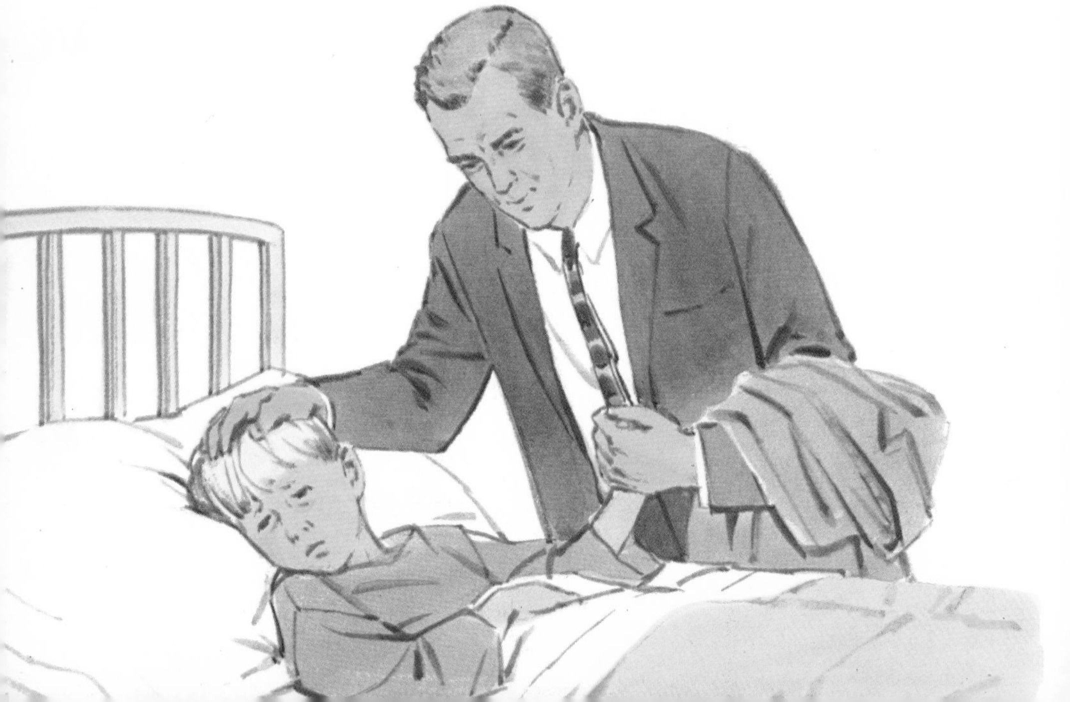

A Keen Idea

Isn't it a good thing that people can't go on being mad forever? By the next day the Spring Street mothers were cross no longer. By the end of two days Miss Mary was ready to make up, too.

"I will forgive you this time if you agree to do as I say," she said. "Lucky will be back home tomorrow, but he can't play baseball. He can't swim. He can't ride his bicycle. I will forgive you if you agree to keep him entertained until his leg is as well as ever again."

After all, those boys and girls were good kids. They were sorry for what had happened. They were sorry that Lucky was going to miss out on the fun. If Janet was the sorriest of all, maybe she should have been, and you know why.

"Agree! Of course we will," she said to Miss Mary. "I will send Lucky a card every day. Isn't that a good idea?"

"Cards by themselves won't do it," said Miss Mary. "A better idea will be to give up some of your own fun to keep him entertained. Go over to call on him every day. Play some games in the house with him and things like that."

"His mom can't stand to have us all there at once," said Buddy. "Maybe we should make out a list telling who is to go today and who tomorrow."

"A good idea," said Miss Mary.

So down they sat on the steps to make out a list and some plans.

By this time it was late afternoon. The paper boy was coming up the walk with the afternoon paper. I don't know why Miss Mary happened to look at the back page before she looked at the front page, but she did. That was a lucky thing for all of them because right there in great big letters was a keen idea.

WORK THE PUZZLES

AND

WIN A PRIZE

WORK THE PUZZLES
AND
WIN A PRIZE

Under those big letters was a puzzle.

PUZZLE 1

Write the four words on paper in the right order, and their first letters will spell another word.

The words under the puzzle told about the prize.

Every day for two weeks there will be a different puzzle on the back page of this paper. Two weeks from today bring your worked-out puzzles to

DAVE'S GAS STATION
Corner of First
and Fox Streets

Then came the catch. There always is a catch in something like this. You never get something for nothing.

> Drive down in the car with your mother or dad. If he or she will buy 5 gallons of gas, you will get a prize.

As things turned out, that catch was not a catch at all. Every dad on Spring Street liked to buy gas from Dave. He had the best station in town.

As soon as Miss Mary showed them the paper, the boys and girls knew just what to do.

"We all love to work puzzles!" shouted Windy. "So we will help Lucky win that prize. We won't take the prize ourselves because we didn't break our legs. Two heads are better than one when it comes to working out puzzles. Here we are with 10 heads if we count Lucky's."

Everyone agreed that it was a keen idea. Every day for the next two weeks some of the gang went over to Lucky's house to help Lucky out. The rest of the gang worked the puzzle for the day at home. Lucky's mother couldn't stand to have them all there at one time.

The trouble with those puzzles was this. Every day they got harder and harder. In the end, they were just hard work and no fun at all. Not one of that gang wanted to see another puzzle as long as he lived.

Of course, those boys and girls had to stick to the job. They couldn't let Lucky down. They had so much trouble with some of the puzzles that their moms and dads started to feel sorry for them. So once in a while some mom or dad would ask a question. Not to tell any answers, but just to get some boy or girl back on the right track! I think that was all right, don't you?

There isn't enough room in this book for all the puzzles, but here are some of the easy ones.

Puzzle 1

Find the 5 things that are wrong with the picture.

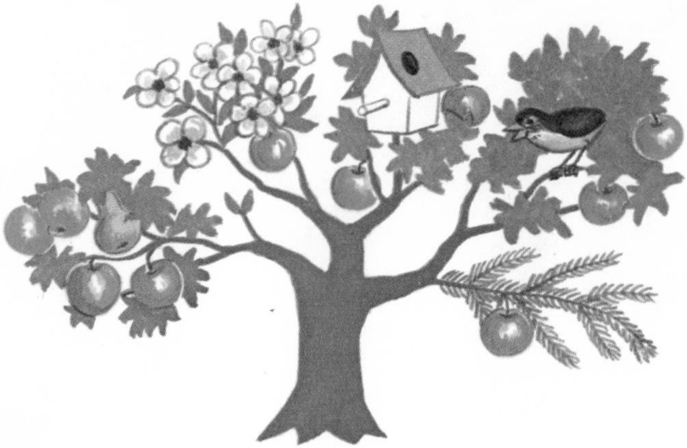

Puzzle 2

ham + bur + glass − lass

+ quarter − quart

Look at the words under the pictures. Write the words on paper, doing what this + and this − tell you to do. You will end with something good to eat.

Puzzle 3

What does this tell you to do?

Puzzle 4

What are the names of the boys and girls?

Puzzle 5

Idea
Cabin
Nose
Actor
Owl
Hand
Moon
Puppy

Write the words on paper in the right order. Their first letters will spell another word. This word will tell you what you are.

A Going-away Present

Days went by. Lucky found out that a broken leg was not so bad after all.

Every day someone rang the doorbell to bring something new to entertain him. Every other night his dad called up to find out how he was getting along. Some of the gang were at the house most of the day. He liked all the attention he was getting.

Before too long, Lucky could get around by himself. If he could not go so fast as the other boys, he could almost.

The day came when the last hard puzzle was all worked out. Lucky put the puzzles into a box, all ready to give to Dave. The plan was to have the girls ride down in the car with Lucky and his mom. The boys would get a head start by going to the gas station on foot.

"Give me a chance to eat breakfast and put on another dress," said Mrs. Masters, when she found the girls at the door on the morning of the great day.

This shows how early that gang got under way.

Of course, there were other boys and girls in Redwood City who had worked out those puzzles and were counting on getting prizes, too. But the Spring Street gang got to the station first.

Lucky got out of the car so fast that he almost forgot about his broken leg. He handed Dave the worked-out puzzles before Dave had a chance to put a gallon of gas into the car.

Maybe Dave was sorry when he saw that broken leg. Anyway, he didn't stop to look the puzzles over.

"I will take your word for it," he said. "The prizes are in a basket on a table in the station. Help yourself to one of them."

Every prize was in a box with a pink ribbon around it.

I hope you don't think that Lucky waited to go home to open that prize. He opened it right then and there while the rest of the gang danced around him.

Then you should have seen what happened. Do you know what a long face is? Well, those were 10 of the longest faces that you have ever seen. Inside that box was a book. Of all things, a book! The words on the paper cover said "A BOOK OF PUZZLES."

It was a good thing that two other cars needed Dave's attention by this time.

"Get going, Mom," whispered Lucky, as his mom helped him into the car while the girls opened the back doors and piled in. "Get out of here fast, and please don't ask me to say 'Thank you' for something I don't want."

His mother, looking around at those disappointed faces, just started the car and didn't say a word. The other boys, looking as mad and as sad as sad-faced owls, just poked along home.

Back again at Lucky's house, the gang just sat around grunting. Not one of them was going to look inside that book.

Then all at once Windy came up with an idea.

"You all know that kid who lives on Front Street. The kid no one likes! Well, he is going to move away soon. We can give him this book for a going-away present."

Before Windy had stopped talking, Lucky and the rest of the gang were on their way to Front Street.

Skip, the kid no one liked, was as pleased as he could be with that book. Of course, no one told him why the gang was giving it to him.

"It will take three days of hard driving to get where we are going," he said. "I can work puzzles when I get tired of looking out the window."

Then he went on to say, "I have a pile of junk Mom won't let me take. Good junk, too! How about taking a look? You can help yourselves to anything."

Before long, everyone in the gang was on his way home with something or other, and Mark was saying, "That kid isn't so bad after all. Maybe it was just us."

That night when Lucky's dad called up and Lucky told him the story, his dad laughed so hard that Lucky saw the funny side of that prize, too.

"I'm sorry you had to give away that book," said his dad. "I was going to bring you the things you need when you and I go fishing together. Now I will take them back and get a puzzle book."

"Dad! Don't do it!" shouted Lucky. "Mom is listening in. Can't you hear her say, 'Enough is enough, but too much is too much of anything?' "

Answers to Puzzles

Page 240	North			
	East	NEWS		
	West			
	South			
Page 244	Puzzle 1	1 pear		
		2 blossoms		
		3 hole in roof		
		4 bird without tail		
		5 pine branch		
	Puzzle 2	hamburger		
Page 245	Puzzle 3	Be sure to watch when you cross a street corner. Stop when you see a bus.		
	Puzzle 4	Henry	Billy	Kitty
		Fanny	Carl	Barbara
		Jack	Buddy	
		Homer	Millicent	
	Puzzle 5	Cabin		
		Hand		
		Actor		
		Moon	CHAMPION	
		Puppy		
		Idea		
		Owl		
		Nose		

All through the Year is the Second Reader of THE HARPER & ROW BASIC READING PROGRAM.

A distinguishing feature of this program is the inclusion, in the basic texts, of various techniques to develop proficiency in independent word attack. The techniques become more comprehensive as the program advances from book to book. The ones used in this book are grouped under six headings: *Picture Dictionary, Words You Can Get by Yourself, Let the Sentences Help You, Let the Syllables Help You, Some Words Have More Than One Meaning,* and *Let the Sound Help You.* Word attack is taught and sharpened through work with picture and context clues, word structure clues, consonant substitution clues, derivatives, compound words, contractions, syllabication, sounds, and multiple meanings.

"Self-help" pages appear at the opening of each unit in the book. Used according to suggestions in the Teacher's Guidebook, they train pupils to attack independently the new words which will appear in the text pages immediately following. Words in the new vocabulary of the unit introduced on the "self-help" pages are underscored on the first two text pages on which they appear in the unit. However, a word appearing more than once on one of these pages is underscored the first time only.

Since pupils master the new vocabulary of the unit before the reading of the text begins, these "self-help" pages lighten the teaching load immeasurably. They help to make pupils self-reliant and contribute to the formation of good study habits. If an underscored word in the text causes difficulty, pupils can turn to the "self-help" pages (as to a dictionary) and help themselves.

WORD LIST

The entire basic vocabulary of the Preprimers, Primer, and First Reader is repeated in *All through the Year*, Second Reader, Strand 1 of THE HARPER & ROW BASIC READING PROGRAM. The following list includes the 249 words that are new to the Second Reader.

Presentation Unit

5 detective
6
7
8
9 step
sad
10 never
11 isn't
say
12 smile
found
13 or
don't
14 tomorrow
soon
15 moved
Mrs.
16 keeps
asks
17 counting
18 lunch
19 seemed
20 whispered
track
21 question
cut
22 doghouse
secret
23
24 garage
bicycle
25 joking
does
26 put
together
27 still
great
28
29 Rusty
grand-
father
30 live
31 us
32

Absorption Unit

33 hero
34
35
36 City
backyard
37 trouble
where
38 fault
39 hated
40 fellow
41 blamed
42 wagging
men
43 hi
wrong
44
45
46 their
47
48
49
50 school
51 postman
52
53 buddies
office
54 wait
55
56 noontime
57
58
59 I'm
60 forgot
61 take
62
63
64
65
66

Presentation Unit

67 mystery
Lake
68
69
70
71 spooky
fall
72 nothing
actors
73 been
gone
74 gang
ever
75 station
wagon
76 cabin
locks
77 key
drives
78 can't
place
79 stands
last
80 popped
leaves
81 care
82 early
83 highway
monkey-
shines
84 turn
didn't
85
86 prove
87 window
open
88
89
90
91 farther
92 burned-
out
bulb
93
94 button
95 crow
swooped
96 pet
pays
97 roof
98 it's
send

Absorption Unit

99 Captain
Sam
100
101
102 side-kick
103 has
grin
104
105 team
win
106 bus
107 kid
108 fans
109
110 champions
111 only
112 field
113 wild
114 November
115 red-letter
116 presents
117
118 tickets
119
120 fingers
121

122
123 touchdown goal
124
125 scored
126
127
128

Presentation Unit

129 remembered
130
131
132
133 winter cold
134 middle noises
135 flakes snow
136 waked sled
137 robe slippers
138 kitchen dust
139 belly flop
140 tops
141 late would
142 puddles floor
143 couldn't grunt
144 breakfast
145 shovel
146 face
147 must
148 took
149 should
150 while
151 clean uneasy
152 dream
153 throw done
154 gave
155 joined goofy
156 always dinner
157
158
159
160 used
161 week
162 brightest

Absorption Unit

163 Alexander
164
165
166 Christmas many
167 name piled
168 most
169 important figures
170 attention
171
172 pleased
173
174
175 life haven't
176 orders pipe
177 marbles
178 seen whiskers
179
180
181 angel wings
182
183 aren't
184 supposed
185
186
187
188
189
190
191 chance
192 spring's winter's

Presentation Unit

193
194
195
196
197 giggling silly
198 moms
199 Princess Blossom
200 hope
201 what's cooking
202 ourselves
203 loud voice
204 minute bring
205 lips
206 course air
207 dresses danced
208 weeds pink
209 doorbell
210 April loves
211 needed table
212 basket because
213 list
214
215 cards
216
217
218 tulips thank
219 hid rang
220 disappointed
221
222 bees passes

Absorption Unit

223
224
225
226 almost summer
227 baseball
228 plans vacation
229 since won't
230 shopping
231 low boost
232 break
233
234 broken
235
236 rub
237 agree entertained
238 sorry
239 puzzles prize
240 Gas
241 buy gallons
242
243
244
245
246
247 box
248
249
250
251 junk
252
253